my
italian
kitchen

my italian kitchen

A FEAST OF FAMILY RECIPES

laura cassai

foreword by GEORGE CALOMBARIS

hardie grant books

MELBOURNE · LONDON

foreword

I am a true believer that it is our past that creates our future. It is the cultural and ethical upbringing that creates the colour, warmth and generosity of who we become. Laura is this and more.

She's a warm young lady who we have fallen in love with on *MasterChef*, not only for her generous cooking but for her humble and hardworking nature. She's a go-getter and an inspiration for the youth of today, and this cookbook is a testament to her hard work and commitment to her family and her food.

Through the *MasterChef* journey, Laura has stayed true to her beliefs. She is an Italian-Australian cook and that's what she does. This book reflects that throughout, with dishes from Sicily, Tuscany and Veneto, where her family comes from, but also dishes from her experiences on *MasterChef*.

I had to stop and think about this, but at the tender age of 19 I wasn't cooking food like Laura is. We can only dream about what she is going to do next.

Lots of love Laura.

George Calombaris

{ laura cassai }

For my three angels and my beautiful family,
I have no words at all. You are the driving force
behind everything I do.

introduction

My love and passion for food was something I was born with. I was fortunate enough to be born into an Italian family, where food was, is and always will be a way of life. Every family gathering was based around food – my mum, Anita, and my two nonnas, Maria and Rosa, in the kitchen preparing feasts, while the kids ran around the house waiting to be fed what we still call the best food we've ever had!

Mum's side of the family comes from Sicily and Veneto, and Dad's comes from Tuscany, which meant I was often getting three cuisines on a plate every dinnertime. And I guess that's where it all started, being taught by the people I love and being inspired by the most traditional regional dishes from my family's Italian roots. Each region has its own recipes, cultural ways and ingredients. There are the fresh seafoods, capers, anchovies and citrus fruits of Sicily, the warm winter polenta stews and cheeses of Veneto, and the most traditional chestnut pancakes of Tuscany. In a sense I had the best of three worlds ...

From the moment I started walking and for as long as I can remember, I would climb onto the bench next to Nonna Maria and want to help make pasta or stir the pot. Over the years, I remember outgrowing the apron that my Nonna made me as a child, the one that she still keeps in her drawer at home. My first real food memory is from when I was six years old, living in the beautiful countryside of Tuscany in Italy, where my Nonna Rosa taught me how to make homemade gnocchi. There was more flour on the floor and in the cracks of the cupboards than in the pasta itself. To this day it is still one of my fondest memories. I look back on my time spent in Italy as a child, and it seems like yesterday. I can still smell the chestnuts cooking over the open fire, feel the damp forest floor while foraging for mushrooms, and taste the crisp and salty potato focaccias we would pick up every morning before school. That was nearly 14 years ago now.

In my teenage years, I was inspired by the time I spent in Italy learning all the traditional cooking techniques. This is the time when I discovered that all I wanted to do was cook. I found food fascinating, everything about it. I began learning more about my Italian heritage, and am still learning today. The traditions and variations in recipes for each region continue to amaze me.

But then along came 2012. It was a rough year for me, one of those years when nothing went right. I was struggling with the demands of Year 12, and ended up in and out of hospital for months with chronic fatigue and glandular fever. I lost my Nonna Rosa in June, one of the most influential women in my life, who has left me with memories and food knowledge to last a lifetime. For her to see me today ... well, I don't think she would have any words. I regained my health and managed to graduate from Year 12. However, on New Year's Eve, I lost my beautiful cousin David in tragic circumstances. It was a huge loss. And then I somehow ended up at university, studying a Bachelor of Health Science ... strangely worlds away from food. But things happen in life, and people regain their direction. In the last few years, I've learnt the hard way that life is precious and you need to take every opportunity that comes your way. For me, that was *MasterChef*.

I now look back at the 18-year-old girl who amazed world-renowned chefs – as well as the judges, Matt Preston, George Calombaris and Gary Mehigan – and, strangely enough, I feel inspired by the girl who first auditioned. I achieved so much in such a short amount of time. I rediscovered my love for a cuisine that defines me. And the show brought out an inner strength I didn't know I had. Being on a reality television show isn't all glamour – it's bloody hard work! Hours of studying, sleepless nights and late-night cook-ups, all to help achieve my goals of being the best that I can be. It's incredibly demanding and stressful, but for all the right reasons. It pushes you to better yourself, and I couldn't be more grateful for the opportunity I was given. It was one of the toughest, yet most rewarding and fulfilling experiences of my life. I got to connect with people and share my story, of a young Italian home cook whose inspiration comes from the apron strings of her mother and two nonnas, Anita, Maria and Rosa.

When I was little I was no kid in a candy store. I was the girl in a bookstore ... and now I'm the girl about to have her own cookbook in a bookstore. Bucket list item 7, check. *My Italian Kitchen* is full of recipes and stories scattered across my life – family ones and my own creations. It's a book of recipes that defines what I'm about: family, love, all things Italian, artichokes and chestnuts, regional recipes, Nonna ... My inspiration for this book comes from my family. I could not have created any of these recipes without their knowledge, their passion for regional Italian food and, most importantly, their love.

Italian food has a way of bringing families together, and that's what I want to highlight in this book: simple, traditional Italian dishes, showcased with only the best seasonal and local produce. Italy is not all about pasta and pizza – it's about the small markets on the side of the road, the wild fruit and vegetables, the annual tomato sauce–making days, Nonna's wooden spoon and Sunday feast of traditional family recipes, sharing meals with your loved ones, large platters and large portions, and the regionalism and seasonality of every dish. It's about family. Oh, and a glass of homemade vino and an espresso coffee. I couldn't imagine growing up in any other family.

I'm sure this is the first chapter of many.

You're forever invited into *My Italian Kitchen*.

Laura.

to start

No meal is complete without a beautiful antipasto plate, and this chapter captures some of my all-time favourites. Artichokes feature strongly, revealing my love for this wonderful vegetable. I've also included some basic but delicious old-school bruschettas and the most traditional, regional chestnut pancakes — only known to Tuscany.

Polenta chips

One of my first memories of having this delicious treat was at the local markets in Italy. There was a man who sold the most incredible polenta chips, and this is where a lot of my inspiration came from. They are a great snack to have before dinner!

INGREDIENTS

- cold leftover **polenta**
- **semolina** for dusting
- **canola oil** for frying
- **sea salt flakes**

METHOD

Cut the cold polenta into chip sizes, and dust the chips with semolina.

Pour canola oil into a small saucepan until it's one-third full and set over a high heat. Check that the oil is hot enough by dropping a small piece of polenta into it – when it turns golden straight away, it's ready. Once hot, add the polenta chips in batches (so they don't all stick together while cooking), and fry until golden.

Drain on paper towel and season with sea salt flakes.

Serve immediately.

Smoked trout and dill croquettes

{ MAKES 20 CROQUETTES }

Fish and dill is a faultless combination – and these croquettes are dead easy to make, and a treat to eat. This is one of those incredibly versatile dishes that is made in many countries all around the world. This recipe of mine is creamy, smoky, full of crunch and so fresh!

INGREDIENTS

- 500 g (1 lb 2 oz) **all-purpose potatoes**
- 30 g (1 oz) **salted butter**, chopped
- 2 tablespoons **plain (all-purpose) flour**
- 250 ml (8½ fl oz/1 cup) **warm milk**
- 1 fillet **smoked trout**, about 150–200 g (5½–7 oz), flaked
- 40 g (1½ oz/1 bunch) **dill**, roughly chopped
- 2 eggs
- 25 g (1 oz/¼ cup) finely grated **Parmigiano Reggiano**
- **sea salt flakes**
- 160 g (5½ oz/2 cups) **fresh breadcrumbs**
- **canola oil** for frying

METHOD

Peel and chop the potatoes into cubes, place them in a saucepan and cover with cold salted water. Bring the potatoes to the boil and cook over a medium heat for a further 15–20 minutes, or until the potatoes are tender.

Meanwhile, to make the béchamel sauce, heat the butter until melted in a small saucepan. Add the flour and cook for a few minutes, until the flour has formed a ball with the butter. Slowly whisk in the milk to ensure there are no lumps, and continue to whisk until all the flour and milk has incorporated. Bring to a slight boil while whisking to ensure the flour has been cooked out. Take off the heat and cool.

Drain the potatoes well, and pass through a sieve into a large bowl. Cool a little, then add the trout, dill, 1 egg, 2 tablespoons of Parmigiano and the béchamel. Season with sea salt and freshly ground black pepper and mix well until all is incorporated.

Roll portions of the mixture into the size of golf balls, or about a quarter cup of mixture.

In a separate bowl, whisk the other egg and season. Combine the breadcrumbs with the remaining cheese in a bowl or tray.

To assemble the croquettes, dip the balls into the egg mixture, then roll them in the breadcrumbs. Set aside.

Pour canola oil into a frying pan until it's approximately 3 cm (1¼ in) deep. Gently fry the croquettes over a medium heat until golden brown all over. Make sure the heat isn't too high as the croquettes will split. Drain on paper towel and serve warm.

Croquettes are best eaten fresh and hot.

Necci

Tuscan chestnut savoury pancakes

{ MAKES 30 LITTLE PANCAKES }

Necci are one of the simplest, yet most magical treats I have ever tasted. The first time I had necci, I was six years old. I was living in Tuscany, where this regional recipe comes from, and I can vividly remember the delicious aftertaste it left in my mouth. With the soft pillow of an ever-so-light chestnut pancake, creamy ricotta and crunchy pancetta, it's a dish that truly captures the essence of the most traditional Italian food.

INGREDIENTS

- 200 g (7 oz/2 cups) **chestnut flour**
- **sea salt flakes**
- **extra-virgin olive oil** for greasing
- 10 thin slices **pancetta**
- 150 g (5½ oz) **fresh ricotta cheese**

METHOD

Whisk the chestnut flour with 300 ml (10 fl oz) of water and a pinch of sea salt in a bowl. Mix until you have a smooth batter.

Lightly grease a non-stick frying pan with olive oil and set over a medium–high heat.

Place 1 tablespoon of batter in the pan for each mini pancake and cook for a couple of minutes, then flip and cook until golden brown. Set aside and keep warm.

Toss the pancetta slices in a frying pan over a high heat until crispy. This should take no more than 5 minutes. Drain on paper towel.

To assemble, place the mini necci on a platter. Spoon on about 1 tablespoon ricotta and top with crunchy pancetta.

To serve as sweet pancakes, top with honey instead of pancetta.

NOTE: CHESTNUT FLOUR CAN USUALLY BE FOUND AT MEDITERRANEAN DELIS OR SUPERMARKETS.

Pasta fritta

One of the things I miss most about living in Italy is the long-table dinners we would have with our neighbours in the small village where we lived. While we patiently waited for the pizzas to be cooked in the scorching wood-fired oven, the women would fry off some pizza dough and serve it with the most incredible fresh cheeses and homemade cured meats. It was so irresistible you would always be full before the pizzas were ready!

INGREDIENTS

- 300 g (10½ oz/2 cups) **00 flour**
- 2 teaspoons **dried yeast**
- pinch of **salt**
- 2 teaspoons **extra-virgin olive oil**, plus extra for coating dough and hands
- 250 ml (8½ fl oz/1 cup) **warm water**
- **canola oil** for frying

METHOD

Mix the dry ingredients together in a large bowl. Add the olive oil and three-quarters of the water, and mix together. Add enough extra water to make a moist, stiff dough.

On a lightly floured surface, gently knead the dough to form a ball. Lightly oil the ball of dough and place in a bowl. Cover with plastic wrap and leave in a warm place for about 1 hour to rest and double in size.

Once the dough has doubled in size, place on a lightly floured surface. Gently knead into a smooth ball. Roll out the dough into a rectangular shape until it is about 2–3 cm (¾–1¼ in) thick.

Cut the dough into slices, approximately 4 cm (1½ in) wide and 6–8 cm (2½–3¼ in) long. Place these on lightly floured trays and leave them for about 3–4 hours, covered with a tea towel (dish towel), to double in size.

Pour canola oil into a frying pan or medium-sized saucepan until it's one-third full, and set over a high heat. Check that the oil is hot enough by dropping a small piece of dough into it – when it turns golden straight away, it's ready. Once hot enough, add a few pieces of dough at a time. Fry until golden and turn over. Cook until both sides are golden, about 4–5 minutes. Drain on paper towel and repeat until all the dough is cooked.

Serve with cold meats (pancetta, salami), cheese and antipasti!

Carciofi ripieni
Stuffed artichokes

{ SERVES 4 AS A STARTER }

With its complexity of flavour and its great versatility, the artichoke is, without doubt, my favourite ingredient. Stuffed artichokes is one of those recipes that will differ from household to household. Every family will stuff them with something different, depending on their flavour preferences or family culinary heritage. The thing I love about this dish is how tender the outer leaves become and how the flesh just melts in your mouth.

INGREDIENTS

- 4 **globe artichokes**
- juice of 1–2 **lemons**, for adding to bowl of water
- 80 g (2¾ oz/1 cup) **fresh breadcrumbs**
- 50 g (1¾ oz/½ cup) finely grated **Parmigiano Reggiano**
- 150 g (5½ oz/1 bunch) **flat-leaf (Italian) parsley**, finely chopped
- 1 **garlic clove**, finely chopped
- ½ long **red chilli**, finely chopped
- **sea salt flakes**
- 80 ml (2½ fl oz/⅓ cup) **extra-virgin olive oil**

METHOD

To prepare the artichokes, cut the tops off so you can see all the layers to the heart (choke). Lightly bash the artichokes on a work surface so that the leaves open up. Squeeze the lemon juice into a bowl of water and place the artichokes in the lemon water to prevent the artichokes from going black.

Mix the breadcrumbs with the Parmigiano, parsley, garlic and chilli, and season with sea salt and freshly ground black pepper. Stuff the filling into the artichokes, ensuring you fill between all the leaves and the centre.

Place the artichokes flat into a saucepan. Drizzle over the olive oil and pour some water into the saucepan until it's approximately 2–3 cm (¾–1¼ in) deep in the saucepan.

Place the lid on and simmer over a low heat for about 30 minutes, until the leaves are tender and they pull away from the heart.

Serve immediately.

Sardine Siciliane agrodolce

Sweet and sour sardines

{ SERVES 4–6 AS A STARTER }

When I'm browsing at the fish markets, sardines are one of the fish varieties that jump out at me instantly. They are so delicate yet so flavoursome. The recipe options are endless with these little fish, whether fried, grilled or baked ... Sardine agrodolce is a very traditional Sicilian dish, a dish I fondly remember my mother making.

INGREDIENTS

- 60 ml (2 fl oz/¼ cup) **extra-virgin olive oil**
- 2 **brown onions**, finely diced
- 40 g (1½ oz/¼ cup) **pine nuts**
- 500 g (1 lb 2 oz) **fresh sardines**, cleaned
- **plain (all-purpose) flour** for dusting
- **balsamic vinegar**
- 1 handful **fresh mint**, roughly chopped

METHOD

To prepare the sweet and sour onions, heat 2 tablespoons of olive oil in a frying pan over a low heat and add the onions. Cook until the onions are tender and caramelised, about 15 minutes.

At the same time, in a separate frying pan, gently toast the pine nuts over a low–medium heat for about 3 minutes, turning the nuts to achieve a good even colour.

To prepare the fish, remove the head and backbone from each sardine, leaving the fish butterflied with the tail intact. Alternatively, purchase butterflied sardines from your local fishmonger.

Heat the remaining olive oil in a frying pan and dust the sardines with a little flour.

Gently cook the sardines in the frying pan over a medium–high heat for about 1 minute on each side, then lightly season.

Lay the sardines on a plate and cover with the caramelised onion.

Add a splash of balsamic vinegar and some chopped mint. Top with the pine nuts.

Arancini

{ MAKES 36 ARANCINI BALLS }

Throughout my childhood, these incredible arancini were always a personal favourite. When we were served up these delicious snacks, I would cut straight into the middle and hope I could make a bigger cheese string than my brother and sister, with the oozing cheesy goodness hiding in the middle of the rice.

INGREDIENTS

- 3 tablespoons **extra-virgin olive oil**
- 1 **onion**, finely diced
- 2 **garlic cloves**, finely chopped
- 800 g (1 lb 12 oz) **tinned chopped tomatoes**
- 1 teaspoon **sugar**
- 50 g (1¾ oz/½ bunch) **basil**, chopped
- 660 g (1 lb 7 oz/3 cups) **arborio rice**
- 3 **chicken stock cubes**
- 3 **eggs**
- 75 g (2¾ oz/½ cup) grated **mozzarella cheese**
- 25 g (1 oz/¼ cup) finely grated **Parmigiano Reggiano**
- 160 g (5½ oz/2 cups) **fresh breadcrumbs**, plus extra if required
- 36 **baby bocconcini (fresh baby mozzarella) balls**, or 36 small cubes **mozzarella cheese**
- **canola oil** for deep-frying
- **sea salt flakes**

METHOD

Heat the olive oil in a medium saucepan and sauté the onion and garlic over a medium heat until they're a light golden colour, about 3 minutes.

Purée the chopped tomatoes before adding them to the pan. Season the mixture with salt and pepper and add the sugar. Add the basil and cook over a medium heat for about 20 minutes. Set aside to cool.

While the sauce is cooking, rinse the rice under cold running water a few times. Pour 1.5 litres (51 fl oz/6 cups) of water into a saucepan, add the rinsed rice and stock cubes, and bring to a boil. Then turn down the heat and continue to cook the rice until tender. This should take about 20 minutes.

Once the rice is cooked, put it in a bowl and allow it to cool down a bit. Once cooled, combine with the eggs, grated cheeses and cooled sauce. If the mixture is too wet to handle, add some breadcrumbs to improve the texture.

So here comes the fun part of this recipe, which is great when children are keen to get involved in the kitchen. Kids have a ball getting their hands stuck into the gooey mix and making the arancini balls.

First up, roll about half a cup of mixture into a ball, stuff the middle with a bocconcini ball or piece of mozzarella, and shape the arancini ball into a pyramid shape.

Continue to do this for the rest of the mixture. You should end up with about 36 arancini balls.

Gently roll each arancino in the breadcrumbs and place on a tray. Refrigerate for 3 hours, or overnight.

Pour canola oil into a saucepan until one-third full. Set over a high heat until the oil is approximately 180°C (360°F). To test whether the oil is ready, place a piece of breadcrumb into the oil – if it turns golden straight away, it's ready. Add the arancini 2 or 3 at a time, depending on the size of the saucepan. They should take 3–4 minutes to cook. Turn throughout the cooking time to ensure they are evenly browned. Drain on paper towel. Continue with the remaining arancini.

Sprinkle with sea salt and serve hot.

Beer-battered artichokes

{ SERVES 6–8 AS A SNACK }

These beer-battered treats are a perfect snack to excite your tastebuds before a beautiful family feast. This batter recipe is light and comes out ever so crispy! And you can use it with any type of vegetable, meat or fish.

INGREDIENTS

- 4–6 **globe artichokes**
- juice of 1–2 **lemons**
- **canola oil** for frying
- **sea salt flakes**

BATTER

- 75 g (2¾ oz/½ cup) **self-raising flour**
- 75 g (2¾ oz/½ cup) **plain (all-purpose) flour**
- 60 g (2 oz/½ cup) **cornflour (cornstarch)**
- **sea salt flakes**
- 250 ml (8½ fl oz/1 cup) **pale ale**

METHOD

To make the batter, whisk the flours, a pinch of sea salt, a pinch of freshly ground black pepper and the pale ale together until there are no lumps.

Clean and cut the artichokes into quarters, removing the stems, outer layers and inner hairy chokes. Squeeze the juice of the lemons into a bowl of water and put the artichoke pieces in the lemon water to prevent the artichokes from going black.

Pour canola oil into a saucepan until approximately one-third full. Set over a high heat until the oil is approximately 180°C (360°F). To test whether the oil is ready, drop a little of the batter into the hot oil – if it turns golden straight away, the oil is hot enough to fry off the artichokes. Dip the artichokes into the batter in batches and gently drop into the hot oil to fry for 4 minutes, or until golden.

Drain the battered artichokes on some paper towel, season with sea salt flakes and serve immediately.

Tomato, buffalo curd and basil bruschetta

{ SERVES 6–8 }

This bruschetta is perfect for breakfast or brunch occasions. Tomato, basil and cheese is the greatest combination of all time, with freshness, acidity, creaminess and crunch. What more could you ask for?! Buffalo curd isn't all that common. I've used it in this recipe, as I think this beautiful ingredient isn't showcased enough. It's the same texture as goat's curd, but not as strong in flavour. It's creamy and goes so well with the freshness of this dish.

INGREDIENTS

- 10–12 thick slices **Ciabatta bread** (page 156)
- 1 **garlic clove**
- 100 g (3½ oz/½ cup) **buffalo curd**
- 4 **roma (plum) tomatoes**, thinly sliced
- 1 large handful **basil**, leaves picked
- **extra-virgin olive oil**
- **sea salt flakes**

METHOD

Toast the ciabatta slices, then rub each side with the garlic clove.

Spread some buffalo curd over the toasted bread, place some tomato slices on top then add some fresh basil leaves.

Drizzle with some olive oil, season with sea salt and crack some black pepper over the top.

NOTE: YOU CAN USE BUFFALO MOZZARELLA BALLS IF YOU CAN'T GET YOUR HANDS ON BUFFALO CURD, WHICH IS AVAILABLE FROM GOOD CHEESE STORES AND SOME DELICATESSENS.

Mushroom and leek bruschetta

{ SERVES 6-8 }

Bruschetta is a dish you simply must have at a family get-together. It's a terrific time-saver as you can do half of the preparation in advance, and just assemble right before your guests are about to arrive. It's quick, easy to make and flavour-packed. Mushroom, leek and thyme ... delicious!

INGREDIENTS

- 1 **leek**, white part only, thinly sliced
- 60 ml (2 fl oz/¼ cup) **extra-virgin olive oil**, plus extra for drizzling
- **sea salt flakes**
- 2 **garlic cloves**, 1 finely diced, 1 whole
- ½ long **red chilli**, finely diced
- 4 large **portobello mushrooms**, thinly sliced
- 1 small handful **thyme**, leaves picked
- 20 g (¾ oz) **salted butter**
- 10–12 thick slices **Ciabatta bread** (page 156)
- thinly shaved **Parmigiano Reggiano** to garnish

METHOD

Preheat the oven to 200°C (390°F).

Place the leek in a baking tray, drizzle with half the olive oil and season with sea salt and freshly ground black pepper, then place in the oven and bake for 20–30 minutes, until tender, sweet and caramelised. Toss halfway through to ensure an even caramelisation.

Pour the remaining olive oil into a frying pan and set over a medium heat. Add the diced garlic and chilli, and sauté for 1 minute. Add the mushrooms and thyme and continue to cook over a medium heat until the mushrooms have cooked through, about 3–5 minutes. Add the butter and season. Set aside.

Toast the slices of bread, then rub each side with the whole garlic clove.

Place the caramelised leek on top of the toasted bread, then the mushrooms and a few shavings of cheese. Drizzle with olive oil and serve.

Tomato, buffalo curd and basil bruschetta

Stuffed zucchini flowers

{ SERVES 12 AS A SNACK OR
6 AS A STARTER }

When I lived in Melbourne, I always looked forward to zucchini season, wanting to be the first to pick all the zucchini flowers in our family garden. They're subtle in flavour yet vibrant and so versatile. Stuffed and fried – ever so simple, yet ever so delicious!

INGREDIENTS

- 12 **zucchini (courgette) flowers**
- 12 large **basil leaves**
- 6 **baby bocconcini balls**, halved
- 6 **marinated anchovy fillets**, halved
- **canola oil** for frying

BATTER

- 75 g (2¾ oz/½ cup) **self-raising flour**, sifted
- 75 g (2¾ oz/½ cup) **plain (all-purpose) flour**, sifted
- 60 g (2 oz/½ cup) **cornflour (cornstarch)**, sifted
- **sea salt flakes**
- 250 ml (8½ fl oz/1 cup) **pale ale**

METHOD

Before you can stuff the zucchini flowers, you will need to clean them. Open up each flower and remove the inside bud.

Stuff each flower with a basil leaf, half a bocconcini ball and half an anchovy fillet.

Twist the top of the flower to seal it and to prevent it from opening when fried.

For the batter, I like to use a really light beer batter as it puffs and crisps, and it's super easy to make.

Combine all the dry batter ingredients (flours, sea salt and some freshly ground black pepper) in a bowl and slowly whisk in the beer. Continue whisking until there are no lumps and you have a smooth batter.

Pour canola oil into a frying pan until it's one-third full and set over a high heat until the oil is approximately 180°C (360°F). Drop a breadcrumb into the oil to test if the oil is ready – if it turns golden straight away, the oil is hot enough. Dip each zucchini flower into the batter and then place into the oil. Fry on each side for no more than 2 minutes, or until the zucchini flowers are golden and crispy.

Drain on paper towel, season and enjoy warm as a snack.

Quail, peach, witlof, prosciutto and buffalo mozzarella salad with balsamic glaze

{ SERVES 4 }

This salad is so simple, and these flavours have been reinvented by so many in so many different ways. I love the sweetness of the peach, the bitterness of the witlof, the smokiness of the quail, the saltiness from the prosciutto and the creaminess of the mozzarella, all brought together by the acidic balsamic glaze.

INGREDIENTS

- 4 **quail**, using only the legs and breasts
- 2 **yellow peaches**, halved and stoned
- 2 **witlof (chicory)**, halved
- **extra-virgin olive oil**
- **sea salt flakes**
- 125 ml (4 fl oz/½ cup) **balsamic vinegar**
- 8 thin slices **prosciutto**
- 2 **buffalo mozzarella balls**, broken into chunks
- 1 small handful **basil leaves**

METHOD

Remove the breasts and legs from each quail. If you don't know how to do this, you can ask your local butcher to help you out. Alternatively, if you want to give it a go yourself, remember that removing the legs and breasts from a quail is exactly like removing them from a chicken. To remove the breast, use a filleting knife or small sharp knife to cut down along the backbone, starting from the top and finishing at the bottom of the quail. Then run your knife under the breast, moving the knife away from you, and carefully remove the breast in one piece. Make sure the wishbone is not attached to the breast. To remove the legs, make a cut from underneath the quail at the join between the leg and back, then follow the joint around. Snap the leg backwards as it makes it much easier to pull apart.

Coat the quail breast and legs, peaches and witlof in olive oil, and season with sea salt and freshly ground black pepper. Over a prepared open fire or barbecue (a chargrill pan can also work), cook the quail for 2 minutes on each side, or until the skin has caramelised and the quail is still a little soft and blushing inside. Rest for 3 minutes under foil.

Add the peaches and witlof to the open fire or barbecue and cook for a few minutes to get char marks. Set aside.

In a small frying pan, heat the balsamic vinegar over a medium heat until it reduces by half. It should be thick and glossy.

In a large serving bowl, place the witlof at the bottom and layer with the quails, peaches, fresh prosciutto and mozzarella chunks. Drizzle over a little balsamic reduction and extra oil, and garnish with basil leaves.

CHAPTER TWO

the garden

Growing up I loved nothing more than collecting beans from Nonna's garden, picking lemons straight off the tree and stuffing only the freshest baby zucchini flowers. There is no greater satisfaction than growing your own fruit and vegetables, seeing them transform from seedlings to plants, then into a delicious dish on the dinner table.

Rolled gnocchi with porcini mushrooms, caramelised onions and crispy sage

{ SERVES 4 }

This dish will always be connected to my fondest memories of Marco Pierre White. I was fortunate enough to cook for Marco while on MasterChef, where he gave me the highest compliment I will probably ever receive in my life. To be told by the father of modern cooking that at my age he couldn't cook a dish to this standard, was truly one of the proudest moments in my life.

INGREDIENTS

- 1½–2 cups **dried porcini mushrooms**
- 1.8 kg (4 lb) **white-fleshed potatoes** (about 8), cut into 1.5 cm (½ in) cubes (I use desiree or toolangi delight potatoes)
- 40 g (1½ oz/1 bunch) **sage**, leaves picked
- 140 ml (4½ fl oz) **extra-virgin olive oil**
- 2 large **brown onions**, finely chopped
- **sea salt flakes**
- 75 g (2¾ oz/½ cup) **00 flour**
- 1 **egg yolk**

METHOD

Cover the porcini with water in a small saucepan over a high heat. Bring to the boil, remove from the heat and allow to sit for 10 minutes until softened. Remove the porcini from the water and finely chop. Set aside.

Cover the potatoes with cold water in a saucepan, salt the water and set over a high heat. Bring to the boil, reduce the heat to medium and allow to gently boil until soft, about 20–25 minutes.

While the potatoes are cooking, make the stuffing. Finely chop half the sage leaves. Pour 2 tablespoons of the olive oil into a frying pan and set over a medium heat. Add the onion, porcini mushrooms and finely chopped sage, and fry until golden, about 5 minutes. Season with sea salt and freshly ground black pepper. Remove from the heat and set aside.

Drain the potatoes and mash. Pass through a drum sieve into a bowl. If you don't have a drum sieve, use a regular sieve or a potato masher to turn the potatoes into a smooth mash. Add the flour, egg yolk and a pinch of salt and stir to combine. Do not overwork the potato dough as it will become very gluey and starchy.

Lay a large piece of plastic wrap on a work surface. Spray with olive oil to prevent sticking. Spread one-quarter of the potato mix onto the plastic in a rectangular shape approximately 10 cm × 28 cm (4 in × 11 in) with a 1 cm (½ in) thickness. Spread one-quarter of the stuffing mix along the length and roll tightly in the plastic wrap. Twist the ends to secure, and seal by tying with cooking string to make a tight, firm roll. Repeat with the remaining mixture, using one-quarter quantities each time to make four rolls.

Bring a saucepan or large deep frying pan of water to the boil over a high heat. Add the potato rolls and cook until set, about 10–12 minutes. Remove from the water and allow to sit for 10 minutes.

Unwrap and cut the rolls into 2 cm (¾ in) thick slices. Pour the remaining olive oil into a frying pan and set over a medium heat. Add the gnocchi slices and fry until lightly browned on both sides. Remove from the frying pan and set aside, keeping warm.

Add the remaining sage leaves to the frying pan and cook until crispy, about 1–2 minutes. Season with sea salt and remove from the heat.

To serve, place the gnocchi slices in a bowl with the crispy sage leaves.

OPTIONAL: RESERVE ABOUT ONE-FIFTH OF THE FILLING FOR THE FINAL PLATING OF THE DISH. REHEAT THE RESERVED FILLING AND SPOON OVER THE FRIED GNOCCHI TO CREATE A SWEETER, JUICIER DISH. SERVE IMMEDIATELY.

Rolled gnocchi with porcini mushrooms, caramelised onions and crispy sage

Pasta finocchi with mollica

{ SERVES 4 }

Growing up, I remember Mum and Dad always wanting to pick the wild fennel on the side of the road. I never understood why, and hated being dragged along to pick it, thinking it was so embarrassing to be seen picking what I called 'weeds' off the side of the road. Oh, was I wrong! Wild fennel has this depth of flavour that really is beyond words. Mollica is a toasted crunchy breadcrumb topping, used as 'poor man's parmesan' back in the old days for those who couldn't afford to buy parmigiano for their pasta.

INGREDIENTS

- 850 ml (28½ fl oz) **Napolitana sauce** (page 166)
- 1 bunch **wild fennel fronds**
- 2 tablespoons **extra-virgin olive oil**
- 2 **garlic cloves**, finely chopped
- 1 long **red chilli**, thinly sliced
- 2–3 **anchovy fillets**, chopped
- 100 g (3½ oz/1 cup) **dry breadcrumbs**
- **sea salt flakes**
- 500 g (1 lb 2 oz) **maccheroncini pasta** (or pasta of your choice)

METHOD

Make the napolitana sauce.

Wash and chop the fennel into 2–3 cm (¾–1¼ in) pieces.

Bring a large saucepan of water to the boil, and boil the fennel for a few minutes until tender, then drain.

Pour half the olive oil into a saucepan over a low–medium heat, add the chilli, the fennel and half the garlic, and season with salt. Slowly fry for 5 minutes until lightly golden. Set aside.

In another saucepan, heat the remaining oil. Add the remaining garlic, the anchovies and the breadcrumbs, and fry over a low heat until the breadcrumbs are golden. Season with sea salt and set aside.

Cook your favourite pasta. I like to use maccheroncini as it goes perfectly with this sauce! Toss the pasta with a little of the tomato sauce, spoon over more tomato sauce, then the fried fennel and breadcrumb mixture *(mollica)*, and serve immediately.

NOTE: YOU CAN ONLY MAKE THIS RECIPE WITH WILD FENNEL. ASK YOUR LOCAL FRUIT SHOP IF THEY CAN GET IT IN OR TRY THE MARKETS. SOME ARE EVEN LUCKY ENOUGH TO FIND IT WHEN FORAGING. IT GROWS LIKE CRAZY IN THE COUNTRY AND ON THE SIDE OF THE ROAD.

Spaghetti with rape (broccoli rabe)

{ SERVES 4 }

Rape, or broccoli rabe, is a hidden gem. I love all things bitter, and this beautiful ingredient's bitterness is incredible. It's such a shame that it's only available for a short time during the year, and isn't commonly known to many.

INGREDIENTS

- 500 g (1 lb 2 oz) **spaghetti**
- 1 bunch **rape (broccoli rabe)**, choose a bunch with more broccoli florets
- 2 tablespoons **extra-virgin olive oil**
- 2–3 **garlic cloves**, thinly sliced
- 1 long **red chilli**, thinly sliced
- **sea salt flakes**
- freshly grated **Parmigiano Reggiano** for serving

METHOD

Bring a large saucepan of salted water to the boil. Add the pasta and cook for 10 minutes or until *al dente*. Drain.

Meanwhile, wash and slice the rape into 3–4 cm (1¼–1½ in) lengths.

Heat the olive oil in a saucepan over a medium heat. Add the garlic and chilli and fry until golden, about 3–5 minutes. Add the rape and sauté for a few minutes, adding a little water. Place the lid on the saucepan and cook for 5–10 minutes until tender. Season with sea salt flakes and freshly ground black pepper.

Toss through the cooked pasta and serve immediately with freshly grated cheese.

NOTE: RAPE (ALSO KNOWN AS BROCCOLI RABE, *CIMA DI RAPA* AND *RAPINI*) IS AVAILABLE FOR A SHORT TIME DURING THE YEAR. MOST GOOD LOCAL FRUIT SHOPS AND MARKETS HAVE IT OR CAN GET IT IN FOR YOU. THERE REALLY IS NO SUBSTITUTE FOR IT ... IT'S VERY TRADITIONAL.

Farfalle pasta with peas, mint, lemon and goat's curd

{ SERVES 4 }

For someone like me, who usually hates mint, this is one of the freshest and most vibrant plates of pasta I can ever have. It's such a beautiful spring dish to make, right when peas are at their best and are ever so fresh, straight out of their pods. The delicious sweet peas, the refreshing flavour of the mint, the tang of the lemon, the creaminess of the goat's curd – the flavour combination is a winner. It's also so quick and easy to make. Enjoy!

INGREDIENTS

- 500 g (1 lb 2 oz) **fresh farfalle pasta**
- 3 tablespoons **extra-virgin olive oil**
- 255 g (9 oz/1⅔ cups) **shelled fresh peas** (frozen peas are fine if fresh aren't available)
- 1 large handful **mint leaves**, reserve some for garnish
- finely grated zest and juice of 1 **lemon**
- **sea salt flakes**
- 50 g (1¾ oz) **goat's curd**

METHOD

Bring a very large saucepan of salted water to the boil. Cook the pasta until *al dente* and then strain.

Heat the olive oil in a saucepan over a medium heat. Add the peas and mint and cook for a few minutes, then deglaze with the juice of the lemon. Season with sea salt and freshly ground black pepper and remove from the heat.

Toss the cooked pasta through the peas. Place in a serving bowl, sprinkle with lemon zest, a few dollops of goat's curd and reserved mint leaves. Serve warm.

Silverbeet and goat's cheese agnolotti with artichokes and pesto

{ SERVES 4 AS A MAIN OR
6 AS A STARTER }

I dedicate this dish to my beautiful Nonna Maria, who won the hearts of so many MasterChef viewers during my time on the show. This recipe is my definition of perfection. It is, without a doubt, Nonna Maria's signature dish. It's often on the menu for lunch or dinner. Well, she makes sure of it, as she knows it's my all-time favourite.

INGREDIENTS

- **Pasta dough** (page 160)
- 75 ml (2½ fl oz) **extra-virgin olive oil**
- 3 **garlic cloves**, crushed
- 1 bunch **silverbeet (Swiss chard)**, thick stalks removed, chopped
- 320 g (11½ oz) **goat's cheese in oil**, drained and crumbled
- **sea salt flakes**
- **semolina** for dusting
- 1 **onion**, finely chopped
- 2 **artichokes**, trimmed and thinly sliced
- 100 g (3½ oz/1 bunch) **basil**, leaves picked

METHOD

Prepare the pasta dough recipe to the step where it has rested for 30 minutes (see page 160).

Meanwhile, to make the pasta filling, pour 2 tablespoons of the olive oil in a frying pan, add one-third of the garlic and all of the silverbeet, and cook over a medium heat, stirring, until the silverbeet has wilted. Remove from the heat, add the goat's cheese, season with sea salt and freshly ground black pepper, and set aside.

Divide the dough into six portions, shaping into discs and dusting with semolina. Feed each disc through a pasta machine, working through the settings until you reach a setting Number 5 or 6, depending on how thin you want it.

Lay one sheet of pasta on a floured work surface, place teaspoon amounts of filling on the sheet, leaving a gap of approximately 5 cm (2 in) between each. Place another pasta sheet over the top and press around the filling mounds to remove any air.

Using an 8.5 cm (3¼ in) cutter, cut around each spoonful of filling to form the agnolotti. Press the edges firmly with a fork. Continue until all the dough and filling have been used. Set the agnolotti aside on a lightly floured tray covered with plastic wrap or a tea towel (dish towel) until ready to cook.

For the artichoke and pesto sauce, place 1 tablespoon of the olive oil in a frying pan and set over a medium heat. Add the onion, remaining garlic and artichoke slices and cook, stirring occasionally, until the artichoke slices are tender, about 10 minutes.

- 50 g (1¾ oz/⅓ cup) **pine nuts**

- 2 tablespoons grated **Parmigiano Reggiano**, plus extra for serving

- 125 ml (4 fl oz/½ cup) **cream**

- 4 slices **pancetta**, chopped

While the artichoke is cooking, process the basil, pine nuts, Parmigiano and 2 tablespoons of olive oil in a food processor until combined. Transfer the pesto sauce to the artichoke mixture, add the cream and allow to cook until warm, stirring to combine. Season with salt and pepper, remove from the heat and set aside until needed.

Bring a large saucepan of salted water to the boil over a high heat. Add the agnolotti and cook until *al dente*, about 2 minutes. Drain.

Meanwhile, in a small frying pan, crisp the pancetta for a few minutes until crunchy.

To serve, place the agnolotti in a bowl, add the artichoke sauce, and sprinkle with crispy pancetta and grated Parmigiano.

NOTE: SILVERBEET IS SUCH AN UNDERVALUED AND OVERLOOKED VEGETABLE. TOO MANY PEOPLE THINK THAT SPINACH HAS MUCH MORE FLAVOUR AND DEPTH, BUT ACTUALLY SILVERBEET IS DELICIOUS WHEN COOKED PROPERLY AND MATCHED WITH THE RIGHT QUALITY INGREDIENTS. SIMPLY SAUTÉ SILVERBEET WITH A LITTLE GARLIC AND A SQUEEZE OF LEMON JUICE, AND THERE IS A PERFECT, QUICK AND EASY SIDE DISH.

Silverbeet and goat's cheese agnolotti with artichokes and pesto

Pesto pasta with roasted tomato, pine nuts and bocconcini

{ SERVES 4 }

This is one of those recipes that I love making when I don't want to spend too much time on dinner. In my house, there's always a jar of pesto in the fridge, which makes this dish even quicker to throw together. And it makes a really tasty meal! Roasting the tomatoes gives a rich depth of flavour, caramelised crunchy bits and a hint of saltiness. This is another perfect cheese, tomato and basil combination.

INGREDIENTS

- 500 g (1 lb 2 oz) **cherry tomatoes**, halved
- **sea salt flakes**
- **extra-virgin olive oil**, about 125–250 ml (4–8½ fl oz/½–1 cup), depending on how wet you want your pesto, plus extra for drizzling
- 40 g (1½ oz/¼ cup) **pine nuts**, plus extra for garnish
- 100 g (3½ oz/1 bunch) **basil**
- 25 g (1 oz/¼ cup) finely grated **Parmigiano Reggiano**
- 2 **garlic cloves**
- 500 g (1 lb 2 oz) **fresh pasta**
- 200 g (7 oz) **bocconcini**, halved or quartered

METHOD

Preheat the oven to 220°C (430°F).

Place the cherry tomatoes on a baking tray. Season with sea salt and freshly ground black pepper, and drizzle with a little olive oil. Bake for approximately 25–30 minutes, or until blistered and caramelised.

Heat the pine nuts in a frying pan over a medium heat until golden in colour. Set aside.

To make the pesto, blitz the basil, pine nuts, Parmigiano, garlic, olive oil, and a pinch of salt and pepper until all smooth and combined. Set aside.

To cook the pasta, bring a large saucepan of salted water to the boil. Add your fresh pasta and gently stir for a minute. Cook until just *al dente* (this should take no more than 4 minutes, depending on the thickness of the pasta).

Toss the cherry tomatoes, pesto and bocconcini pieces through the pasta and scatter a few pine nuts over the top to serve.

Cavolo nero, borlotti beans, polenta and sausages

{ SERVES 4-6 }

When I was growing up, one of my biggest food heroes was Antonio Carluccio. I still remember seeing him cooking a version of this delicious recipe on one of his cooking shows, and this is my take on the classic dish. I love everything about this meal – its simplicity, the ingredients used and its heartiness.

INGREDIENTS

- 1 bunch **cavolo nero (Tuscan cabbage)**
- 2 tablespoons **extra-virgin olive oil**
- 1 **brown onion**, finely chopped
- 2–3 **garlic cloves**, chopped
- 2 **sage sprigs**, roughly chopped
- **sea salt flakes**
- 400 g (14 oz) **tomatoes**, chopped, or 400 g (14 oz) **tinned chopped tomatoes**
- 500 g (1 lb 2 oz) **fresh borlotti beans**, shelled
- 6 large **Italian pork sausages**
- **Polenta** (page 164)

METHOD

Remove the stems from the cavolo nero and chop.

Heat the olive oil in a large deep saucepan and add the onion, garlic and sage. Season with sea salt and freshly ground black pepper. Sauté until translucent and tender, about 3–4 minutes.

Add the tomatoes and borlotti beans, and cook over a low heat until the tomatoes start to break down. Add the cavolo nero and continue cooking for 20 minutes or so. Season lightly with sea salt and pepper.

In a separate heated frying pan, brown the sausages over a medium–high heat. Transfer the sausages to the saucepan with the bean mixture and continue cooking for a further 15 minutes until the sausages have cooked through and the beans are tender.

Serve with polenta.

Heirloom carrots with fennel and orange dressing

{ SERVES 4 }

Fennel and orange really is a winning combination, and this delicious side dish is a quick and easy accompaniment for a perfect roast! Heirloom carrots are such beautiful ingredients to use. I think more than anything I love their vibrant colours!

INGREDIENTS

- 8–10 **heirloom carrots**, trimmed
- 80 ml (2½ fl oz/⅓ cup) **extra-virgin olive oil**
- juice of 2 **oranges**
- 1 tablespoon **honey**
- 2 tablespoons **fennel seeds**
- **sea salt flakes**

METHOD

Preheat the oven to 200°C (390°F).

Cut the carrots in half lengthways.

Put the carrots in a bowl with the olive oil, orange juice, honey and fennel seeds, and season with sea salt and freshly ground black pepper. Toss to combine.

Place on a baking tray lined with baking paper and put in the oven for 30 minutes, until the carrots are tender.

Serve in a large bowl.

Tomato, buffalo mozzarella and basil pizza

{ SERVES 6–8 }

When I was in charge of the toppings on family pizza night, I was always trying to come up with something different and complicated. Though this is one of the simplest pizza combinations there is, it's also one of the best – and it's still one of my all-time favourites.

INGREDIENTS

- 1 **Pizza base** (page 158)
- **extra-virgin olive oil** for drizzling
- 5 large **roma (plum) tomatoes**, thinly sliced
- 3 **buffalo mozzarella balls**
- 100 g (3½ oz/1 bunch) **basil**, leaves picked
- **sea salt flakes**

METHOD

Preheat the oven to 220°C (430°F).

Place the pizza base on a baking tray or pizza stone. Drizzle some olive oil over the top of the base. Add the tomato slices, and break up some mozzarella and scatter over the tomato. Top with basil leaves, season with sea salt and freshly ground black pepper, and drizzle with more olive oil.

Bake for 15 minutes or until the pizza base is crisp.

Potato, caramelised onions and rosemary oil pizza

{ SERVES 6–8 }

I would always want this as my focaccia topping during our time in Tuscany. It's a beautiful combination that works well even if you ditch the pizza base. Just toss the onions and oil through roast potatoes – it's absolutely stunning.

INGREDIENTS

- 3 **potatoes**
- 105 ml (3½ fl oz) **extra-virgin olive oil**
- 2 **red onions**, thinly sliced
- 2 **rosemary sprigs**
- **sea salt flakes**
- 1 **Pizza base** (page 158)

METHOD

Preheat the oven to 220°C (430°F).

Thinly slice the potatoes on a mandoline and place the slices in a bowl of water to prevent them from going black.

Heat 60 ml (2 fl oz/¼ cup) of the olive oil in a saucepan. Add the onion slices and cook over a very low heat for 15–20 minutes until they are soft and lightly caramelised. Set aside.

Finely chop the rosemary, mix with 3 tablespoons of olive oil in a small bowl and season with sea salt and freshly ground black pepper.

Place the pizza base on a baking tray or pizza stone. To assemble, drizzle some of the rosemary oil on the pizza base. Layer the potato slices all over the pizza, top with the onion and drizzle with more of the rosemary oil.

Bake for 15–18 minutes, until the pizza base is crisp.

Tomato, buffalo mozzarella
and basil pizza

Potato, caramelised onions and rosemary oil pizza

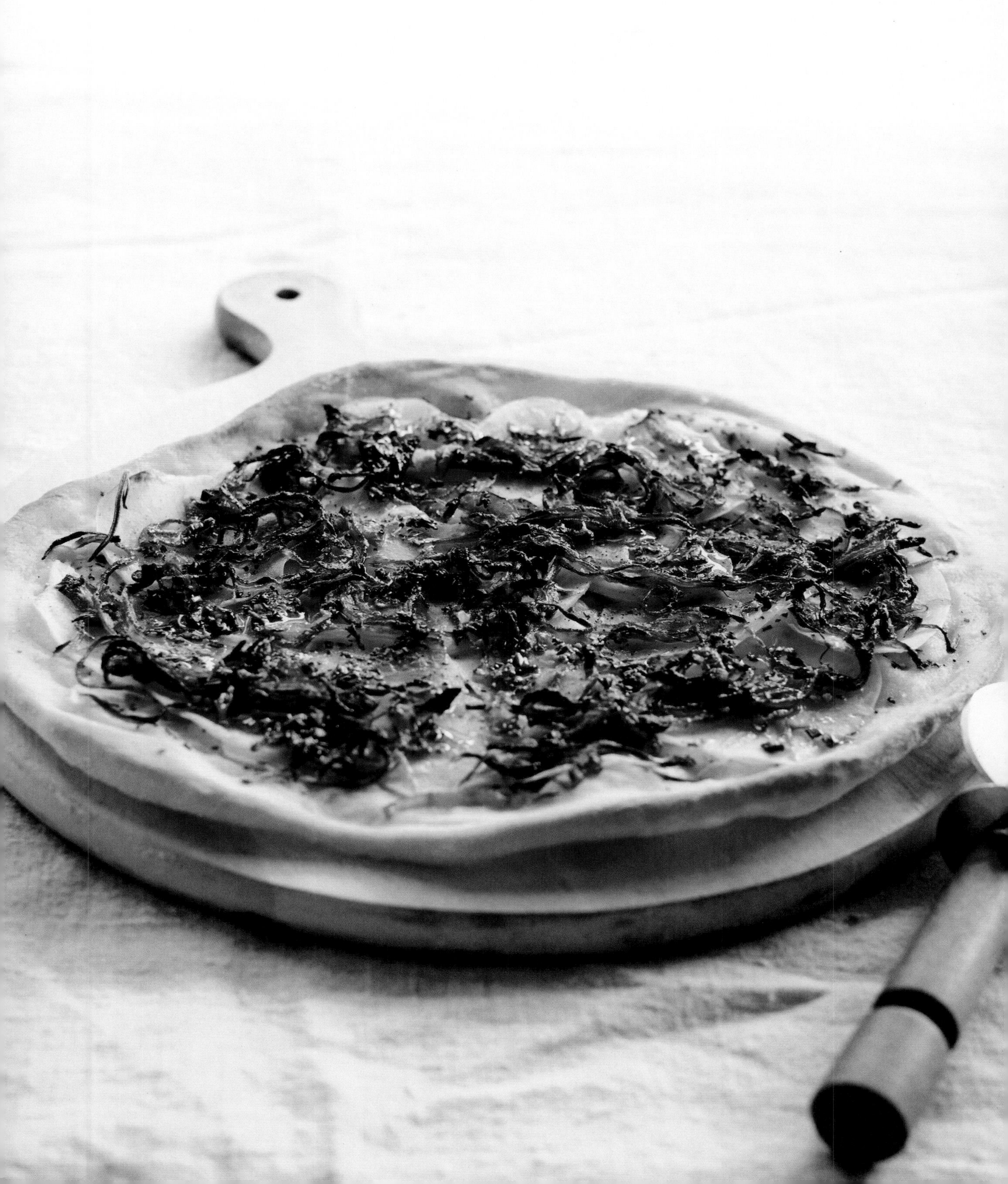

Gorgonzola, prosciutto, rocket and pesto pizza

{ SERVES 6-8 }

This is a beautiful and pretty fancy topping to have on your homemade pizza. It's such a classic combination, with the creaminess and bite from the gorgonzola, the saltiness of the delicate prosciutto and the peppery yet refreshing kick of the rocket.

INGREDIENTS

- 1 **Pizza base** (page 158)
- 2 tablespoons **Pesto** (page 167)
- 1½ tablespoons **extra-virgin olive oil**, for drizzling
- 100 g (3½ oz) **gorgonzola cheese**
- 100 g (3½ oz) **prosciutto**, thinly sliced
- 1 handful **rocket (arugula)**
- **balsamic vinegar** for drizzling

METHOD

Preheat the oven to 220°C (430°F).

Place the pizza base on a baking tray or pizza stone. Drizzle over the pesto and enough olive oil to ensure the entire pizza base is lightly covered.

Break the gorgonzola into small bits and sprinkle over the pizza, then roughly lay slices of prosciutto on top.

Bake the pizza for 15–18 minutes, remove from the oven and scatter the rocket leaves on top. Drizzle with a little more olive oil and splash with balsamic vinegar. Crack some black pepper on top and serve.

Mushroom risotto

{ SERVES 6 }

A risotto is one of the most traditional Italian dishes, but for some reason people find it difficult to make. It should be creamy, smooth and still have an al-dente bite to the rice. Mushroom risotto is my favourite, and I love using all different varieties of mushrooms when they are in season. You can use this base recipe for most risottos – just replace the mushrooms with your own flavour combinations!

INGREDIENTS

- 6 **dried porcini mushrooms**
- 60 ml (2 fl oz/¼ cup) **extra-virgin olive oil**
- 1 **brown onion**, finely chopped
- 3 **garlic cloves**, 2 chopped and 1 sliced
- 440 g (15½ oz/2 cups) **arborio rice**
- 250 ml (8½ fl oz/1 cup) **white wine**
- 1.5 litres (51 fl oz/6 cups) hot **Chicken stock** (page 165)
- 250 g (9 oz) **mixed mushrooms** (portobello, button, pine)
- **sea salt flakes**
- 30 g (1 oz) **salted butter**
- 2–3 tablespoons grated **Parmigiano Reggiano**

NOTE: MAKING YOUR OWN STOCK FOR RISOTTO GIVES THE END PRODUCT A MUCH BETTER FLAVOUR. HOWEVER, IF YOU DON'T HAVE A LOT OF TIME YOU CAN ALWAYS USE PACKET STOCK.

METHOD

Boil the kettle and pour the boiling water into a heatproof bowl with the dried porcini mushrooms to soak for about 10 minutes until they are soft. Drain but reserve the liquid as it has a beautiful porcini mushroom flavour. Roughly chop the mushrooms.

Heat 2 tablespoons of the olive oil in a frying pan, add the onion, chopped garlic and rehydrated porcini mushrooms, and cook slowly over a low heat for approximately 10 minutes until both the onions and garlic are tender.

Turn up the heat to medium, add the rice and stir until the rice begins to toast and becomes translucent, approximately 1–2 minutes.

Add the wine to the rice and keep stirring until the rice absorbs all the wine.

Turn down the heat to a simmer once all the wine has been absorbed, and then add the first ladle of hot stock to the rice. Continue stirring and once the rice has absorbed all the stock, add another ladleful of stock. Continue this process for approximately 20 minutes, or until the rice is cooked. It should be soft but still have a slight bite to it.

Meanwhile, at the same time as the rice is cooking, heat a separate frying pan with 2 tablespoons of olive oil, and sauté the sliced garlic over a medium heat for a minute. Add the mixed mushrooms and sauté until almost cooked, about 5 minutes. Add a little of the porcini liquid for extra flavour. After about 15 minutes of cooking the risotto, add the mushrooms so they cook with the rice for the last 5 minutes of cooking time.

Season to taste with sea salt and freshly ground black pepper, then add the butter and Parmigiano and continue to stir until all the butter has dissolved.

Take off the heat, cover with a lid and leave for a few minutes. This makes the rice creamy, the way it should be served.

the sea

Thoughts of seafood bring back the fondest of childhood memories. The icy mornings fishing on the jetty, picking up kilos of mussels from the dock after the morning catch, and the warm afternoons, collecting cockles down in Goolwa with my family, then returning home at the end of the day with the freshest of seafood for a night's feast.

Fire-grilled fish and seafood

{ SERVES 6 }

Fresh seafood is often at its best when cooked simply. One of my favourite ways of cooking fish and other seafood is just grilled over a fire or barbecue with a squeeze of fresh lemon juice. It's quick and easy, and the simple, honest flavours are magnificent. In this recipe, I use a basic but delicious marinade to complement the fish and seafood. Some people are nervous about cooking with seafood, as sometimes the preparation can be a little tricky. Your local fishmonger can always do this for you – it may cost a little extra, but it's often really worthwhile.

INGREDIENTS

- 2 long **red chillies**, finely diced
- 150 g (5½ oz/1 bunch) **flat-leaf (Italian) parsley**, finely chopped
- 1 **garlic clove**, finely chopped
- 60 ml (2 fl oz/¼ cup) **extra-virgin olive oil**, plus extra for coating
- **sea salt flakes**
- 4 **squid**
- 2 **baby snapper** (or any other small ocean fish), cleaned and scored
- 12 **king prawns (shrimp)**, kept whole
- 12 **sardines**, cleaned and gutted
- 6 **baby octopus**
- 6 **scampi**
- 6 **lemons**, cut into wedges, for serving

METHOD

Heat your barbecue or open-fire grill.

In a small bowl, mix together the chilli, parsley, garlic and olive oil. Season with sea salt and freshly ground black pepper. This will be your marinade to baste over some of the seafood as it is cooking.

To clean the squid, gently pull the tentacles away from the tube (the intestines should come away at the same time). Remove the intestines from the tentacles by cutting under the eyes, then remove the beak if it remains in the centre of the tentacles by using your fingers to push up the centre. Pull away the quill (the transparent cartilage) from inside the body and remove. Remove and discard any white membrane. Under cold running water pull away the skin from the tube. Cut the squid into rings, keeping the tentacles and wings.

Coat all the fish and seafood with a touch of oil to prevent them from sticking while cooking.

The baby snapper are going to take the longest to cook, around 4–5 minutes on each side, so place the fish on the hot barbecue or grill first.

Once the fish has about 4 minutes to go and has been turned, place all the other seafood onto the barbecue or grill, and cook for 2 minutes on each side, or until cooked through. Baste the prawns, sardines, squid, octopus and scampi with the marinade while cooking. You can use a knife to check if everything is cooked through. Just make a slit into the thickest part of each piece of seafood to ensure it's ready.

Once cooked, place all the seafood onto a large platter and serve with lemon wedges.

NOTE: SCORING THE FISH ENSURES IT COOKS MORE EVENLY, AND ALLOWS THE FLAVOURS TO GET INTO THE FLESH TO GIVE THE DISH A MUCH MORE COMPLEX FLAVOUR.

Linguine con le vongole

{ SERVES 4 }

One of my favourite things to do as a family is to go down to Goolwa, on the beautiful coast south of Adelaide, to get the freshest cockles you could ever find. It's amazing to see kilometres of shoreline filled with people digging for cockles. This recipe is the definition of fresh – from ocean to plate in just a few hours!

INGREDIENTS

- 4 **roma (plum) tomatoes**
- 1 tablespoon **extra-virgin olive oil**
- 1 **onion**, finely diced
- 2 **garlic cloves**, finely chopped
- 1 long **red chilli**, finely chopped
- 60 ml (2 fl oz/¼ cup) **white wine**
- 1 kg (2 lb 3 oz) fresh **cockles/clams (vongole)**, rinsed
- **sea salt flakes**
- 1 handful **flat-leaf (Italian) parsley**, roughly chopped
- 600 g (1 lb 5 oz) **fresh linguine**

METHOD

To prepare the tomatoes, boil the kettle and pour the boiling water in a heatproof bowl. Score a cross in the base of each tomato and put them in the bowl of hot water. Leave the tomatoes in the bowl until the skin starts to peel away, about 30 seconds. Remove the tomatoes from the bowl and peel away the skin, then slice and finely dice.

Bring a large saucepan of salted water to the boil.

Meanwhile, heat the olive oil in a large saucepan over a medium heat. Add the onion, garlic and chilli and sauté until soft and lightly coloured, about 3–5 minutes.

Add the tomatoes and cook for a few minutes, then deglaze the pan with the white wine.

Add the cockles, put a lid on the saucepan and cook, covered, for about 5 minutes, until all the cockle shells have opened. (Discard any cockles that have not opened.) Season lightly with sea salt (as cockles can be quite salty). Add some freshly ground pepper and garnish with chopped parsley.

Add the linguine to the boiling water and cook for 3–4 minutes until *al dente*. Drain and toss with the cockles.

Scampi with anchovy butter, roasted garlic cream, scampi roe and pickled cabbage

{ SERVES 4 }

I think this recipe is a testament to how far I have come as a cook over the past few years. I look back and think how crazy it is that I am now able to create dishes like this one. In this recipe, I have used very simple ingredients, but have gone out of my way to extract flavours from each individual ingredient in a very refined way, again inspired by my Italian heritage.

INGREDIENTS

- 1 **garlic bulb**
- 1 tablespoon **grape seed oil**, plus extra for frying
- 4 **scampi**
- 125 ml (4 fl oz/½ cup) **cream**
- 60 g (2 oz) **anchovy fillets**
- 80 g (2¾ oz) **salted butter**, cubed
- 100 g (3½ oz) **pearl barley**

METHOD

Preheat the oven to 180°C (360°F).

Drizzle the garlic with grape seed oil, wrap it in foil and place it in the oven to roast until soft, about 30 minutes.

Meanwhile, prepare the scampi. Slice the scampi in half lengthways and remove the heads (reserve these for later). Reserve the roe for garnish.

Remove the garlic from the oven and peel the cloves. Process the roasted garlic cloves and the cream in a food processor until smooth and combined. Season and set aside.

Process the anchovy fillets and butter in a food processor until smooth and well combined. Set aside.

Place the pearl barley in a saucepan, cover with water and set over a high heat. Bring to the boil, reduce the heat and allow to simmer until the barley is cooked, about 25 minutes. Remove from the heat and drain.

Spread the cooked barley on a baking tray and place in the oven to dry, about 10 minutes.

- 60 ml (2 fl oz/¼ cup) **extra-virgin olive oil**

- 100 ml (3½ fl oz) **white vinegar**

- 80 g (2¾ oz/⅓ cup) **caster (superfine) sugar**

- 100 g (3½ oz) **red cabbage**, finely chopped

- **baby basil** (or any other micro herb)
  to garnish

- **fennel seeds** to garnish

Heat the olive oil in a frying pan, add the scampi heads and fry over a low–medium heat for about 10–15 minutes to get a beautiful infused scampi oil. Strain, discarding the heads, and set aside.

Meanwhile, mix the vinegar, sugar and 50 ml (1¾ fl oz) of water in a saucepan and bring to the boil over a high heat. Place the cabbage in a bowl, pour over the boiling liquid and set aside to pickle.

Pour grape seed oil into a small saucepan until it's one-third full, and set over a high heat until the oil reaches 180°C (360°F). Test the oil by throwing in a breadcrumb – when it turns golden straight away, the oil is ready. Add the dried, cooked barley in batches and fry until golden. Remove from the oil using a slotted spoon and set aside on paper towel.

Place the anchovy butter in a frying pan and set over a medium heat. Fry the scampi halves in the pan, basting with the butter until cooked through, about 1 minute.

To serve, sprinkle plates with the fried barley. Add 2 scampi halves to each plate. Add some garlic cream and drizzle with infused oil. Drain the pickled cabbage and scatter over the plates. Season and garnish with sweet baby basil, fennel seeds and scampi roe.

NOTE: SCAMPI ARE DELICATE AND CREAMY SHELLFISH THAT ARE SMALLER THAN A CRAYFISH AND LARGER THAN A PRAWN (SHRIMP). YOU CAN SUBSTITUTE PRAWNS FOR SCAMPI, BUT YOU WILL FIND PRAWNS AREN'T AS CREAMY.

Scampi with anchovy butter, roasted garlic cream, scampi roe and pickled cabbage

Lobster broth with lobster and tomato ravioli

{ SERVES 4-6 }

I would like to dedicate this recipe to my late Nonna Rosa, one of the biggest influences in my life. For as long as my memory goes back, every single family gathering started with a bowl of brodo (chicken soup) with homemade ravioli. I re-invented this dish on MasterChef for Marco Pierre White, in memory of my nonna.

INGREDIENTS

- **Pasta dough** (page 160)
- 3 tablespoons **extra-virgin olive oil**
- 2 **carrots**, roughly chopped
- 1 **onion**, roughly chopped
- 1 × 3 cm (1¼ in) piece **ginger**, roughly chopped
- 1 **garlic clove**, roughly chopped
- 45 g (1½ oz/½ bunch) **coriander (cilantro) roots**, roughly chopped
- 2 **lobsters**, blanched, tails removed and all shells and heads put aside
- 125 ml (4 fl oz/½ cup) **white port**
- 6 **roma (plum) tomatoes**, 4 roughly chopped, 2 finely chopped
- **sea salt flakes**
- **coriander (cilantro) leaves** to garnish

METHOD

Prepare the pasta dough recipe to the step where it has rested for 30 minutes.

Pour 1 tablespoon of the olive oil into a saucepan and set over a high heat. Add the carrot, the onion, ginger, garlic and coriander roots, and fry for 1–2 minutes. Add the lobster head and shells, and fry until orange. Add the port and heat for 1 minute to cook off the alcohol. Add 4 roughly chopped tomatoes and fry for 1 minute. Add 1.5 litres (51 fl oz/6 cups) of water and bring to the boil. Allow the broth to continue to boil for about 45 minutes until reduced. Remove from the heat, strain and set aside, keeping warm.

Finely dice the lobster tail meat. Pour the remaining olive oil into a frying pan and set over a medium heat. Add the lobster meat and the 2 finely chopped tomatoes, then season with sea salt and freshly ground black pepper and cook until the lobster is just cooked through. Remove from the heat and set aside to cool.

Divide the pasta dough into four portions. Pass the dough through a pasta machine to the thinnest setting. Lay one sheet of dough on a floured work surface. Place 1 tablespoon amounts of lobster filling along the dough, leaving a gap between each, approximately 8 cm (3¼ in). Top with another layer of dough and gently press around the filling to seal. Using a 6.5 cm (2½ in) pastry cutter, cut out the ravioli. Repeat with the remaining dough and filling until you've made 20 ravioli.

Bring a large saucepan of water to the boil over a high heat. Add the ravioli and cook until *al dente*, about 3 minutes. Remove from the water using a slotted spoon.

To serve, place the ravioli in individual bowls and pour over the lobster broth. Garnish with coriander leaves and season with sea salt and freshly ground black pepper.

Puttanesca

{ SERVES 4 }

I'm a massive lover of capers and anchovies, so this recipe is always a favourite of mine around dinnertime. While I was living in Melbourne for MasterChef, I had pasta puttanesca probably every second night. I wouldn't be able to wait for the pasta to be ready, so I'd eat half the anchovies straight out of the jar with a slice of toasted bread.

INGREDIENTS

- 350 g (12½ oz) baby **roma (plum) tomatoes**, halved
- **sea salt flakes**
- 2 tablespoons **extra-virgin olive oil**, plus extra for drizzling
- 1 **onion**, finely diced
- 3 **garlic cloves**, finely chopped
- 2 tablespoons **baby capers**, rinsed and squeezed dry
- 6–8 **anchovy fillets**
- ½–1 long **red chilli**, thinly sliced
- 100 g (3½ oz) **kalamata olives**, pitted
- 50 g (1¾ oz/½ bunch) **basil**, leaves picked
- **sea salt flakes**
- 500 g (1 lb 2 oz) **fresh farfalle pasta** (or pasta of your choice)

METHOD

Preheat the oven to 220°C (430°F).

Place the halved tomatoes on a baking tray, season with sea salt flakes and freshly ground black pepper, then drizzle with some olive oil. Toss to ensure all the tomatoes are coated, place in the oven and bake for 20–30 minutes, until blistered and roasted.

Pour 2 tablespoons of olive oil into a frying pan over a medium heat and sauté the onion, garlic, capers, anchovy fillets and chilli until golden. (Use a half or a whole long red chilli, depending on how spicy you want the sauce.)

Add the roasted tomatoes, olives and basil and toss gently. Season the sauce with sea salt and freshly ground black pepper.

Cook the pasta in boiling salted water until *al dente*, about 3–4 minutes. Strain the pasta and toss through the sauce.

Fisherman's stew

{ SERVES 4 }

This is a dish I created for Heston Blumenthal. I wanted to showcase the depth of flavour you can get out of the whole fish, using all the bits from head to tail. The broth for this stew is just out of this world. It's so packed with flavour, it takes me back to sitting on a dock in Italian coastal towns. It's fresh from the ocean, straight to your plate, and served with crusty bread to soak up all the incredible flavours.

INGREDIENTS

- 10 **raw prawns (shrimp)**
- 140 ml (4½ fl oz) **grape seed oil**
- 1 **onion**, roughly chopped
- 1 **leek**, white part only, roughly chopped
- 2 **carrots**, roughly chopped
- 3 **garlic cloves**, 2 roughly chopped, 1 whole
- 2 **rainbow trout**, cleaned and filleted, bones reserved
- 2 **tomatoes**, roughly chopped
- 1 litre (34 fl oz/4 cups) **fish stock**
- **sea salt flakes**
- 8 **sardines**, cleaned and filleted
- 12 slices **Ciabatta bread** (page 156)
- finely grated **lemon zest** to garnish
- finely grated **lime zest** to garnish
- **flat-leaf (Italian) parsley** to garnish

METHOD

Preheat the oven to 220°C (430°F).

Peel the prawns, leaving the tails intact. Reserve the shells for the stew and the heads for the infusing oil. Cut the prawns in half lengthways and devein. Set aside.

To make the stew, pour a good drizzle of the grape seed oil in a saucepan over a high heat. Add the onion, leek, carrots and roughly chopped garlic and cook until browned, about 3–4 minutes. Add the trout bones, reserved prawn shells and tomatoes and cook until browned, a further 5–8 minutes. Add the stock, bring to the boil, and allow to boil for 30 minutes. Remove from the heat, strain, season with sea salt and freshly ground black pepper and set aside, keeping warm.

Meanwhile, pour 80 ml (2½ fl oz/⅓ cup) of the grape seed oil into a frying pan and set over a medium heat. Add the reserved prawn heads and cook until the oil is flavoured, about 5 minutes. Remove from the heat and strain, reserving the prawn oil.

Return the frying pan to a medium heat, add the prawn meat and the remaining grape seed oil and cook, turning halfway, until just cooked through, about 2–3 minutes. Remove from the heat, season and set aside.

Cut about 2 cm (¾ in) of the flesh off at the tail end of the trout fillets, leaving the skin intact. Roll up the trout fillets, using the tail skin to seal the fillet in place and place upright on a lined baking tray. Bake until almost cooked through, about 3 minutes. Add the sardines to the tray and bake until cooked through, about another minute. Remove from the oven, season and set aside.

Cook the bread slices on a hotplate over a high heat, pressing down and turning. Remove from the plate, rub with the garlic clove and set aside.

To serve, place a trout fillet in the centre of each serving bowl. Place the sardines and prawns around the trout. Pour the stew over the seafood, drizzle with prawn oil and garnish with the zest and parsley. Serve with the garlic-rubbed crusty bread.

Beccafico

This is such a classic Sicilian dish, with its pine nuts, capers, anchovies and currants. I have enjoyed this dish from a young age, always with a fresh and crunchy fennel and orange salad alongside it.

INGREDIENTS

- 4 × 150 g (5½ oz) **garfish fillets**
- **sea salt flakes**
- 1–2 tablespoons **extra-virgin olive oil**

STUFFING

- 3 tablespoons **extra-virgin olive oil**
- 1 **onion**, finely chopped
- 1 **garlic clove**, finely chopped
- 40 g (1½ oz/¼ cup) **pine nuts**
- 3 tablespoons **capers**, rinsed and squeezed dry
- 2 tablespoons **currants**, chopped
- 2 **anchovy fillets**, finely chopped
- 25 g (1 oz/⅓ cup) **fresh breadcrumbs**
- 1 large handful **flat-leaf (Italian) parsley**, finely chopped

FENNEL AND ORANGE SALAD

- 1 **bulb fennel**, trimmed and thinly sliced
- 1 **orange**, peeled and cut into segments, membrane removed
- 2 teaspoons **white-wine vinegar**
- 1 tablespoon **extra-virgin olive oil**

METHOD

Preheat the oven to 220°C (430°F).

To make the stuffing, heat the olive oil in a frying pan over a medium heat. Add the onion and garlic, and sauté until translucent, about 3 minutes. Add the pine nuts, capers, currants and anchovies and cook until the currants have softened, about 3 minutes. Season with sea salt and freshly ground black pepper. Add the breadcrumbs and parsley and stir to combine. Remove from the heat and set aside.

Lay the garfish fillets flat on a chopping board, skin side down. Season with sea salt and freshly ground black pepper and cover each with approximately 2 tablespoons of stuffing. Roll the fillets and secure with a toothpick.

Pour 1–2 tablespoons of olive oil in a frying pan and set over a medium heat. Add the rolled fillets and cook until the skin is sealed, about 2 minutes. Transfer the fillets to the oven until cooked through, about 7–8 minutes. Remove from the oven and set aside.

Meanwhile, to make the salad, toss the fennel, orange, vinegar and olive oil in a bowl until combined. Season to taste.

Serve the garfish fillets with salad on the side.

Seared yellowfin tuna with chestnuts and salsa verde

{ SERVES 4 }

The first time I made this, I think I blew myself away with how much flavour I could pack into such a delicate dish. I learnt that chestnuts and tomatoes complement each other perfectly – and the rest of the ingredients in this dish work incredibly well together, too.

INGREDIENTS

- 10 **chestnuts**, about 160 g (5½ oz)
- 40 ml (1¼ fl oz) **extra-virgin olive oil**
- 2 tablespoons **capers**, drained, rinsed and squeezed dry
- 4 × 4 cm (1½ in) thick **yellowfin tuna steaks**
- **sea salt flakes**
- 3 **radishes**, thinly sliced on a mandoline
- **baby basil leaves** to garnish
- finely grated **orange zest** to garnish
- finely grated **lemon zest** to garnish

SALSA VERDE

- 40 g (1½ oz/½ bunch) **coriander (cilantro)**
- 75 g (2¾ oz/½ bunch) **flat-leaf (Italian) parsley**
- 40 g (1½ oz/½ bunch) **dill**
- 1 **garlic clove**
- 125 ml (4 fl oz/½ cup) **extra-virgin olive oil**

TOMATO REDUCTION

- 1 tablespoon **extra-virgin olive oil**
- 2 **French shallots**, finely chopped
- 6 **anchovy fillets**, finely chopped
- 8 **cherry tomatoes**, halved, plus extra to garnish
- 60 ml (2 fl oz/¼ cup) **red-wine vinegar**

METHOD

Preheat the oven to 220°C (430°F).

Score the chestnuts and place on a baking tray. Place in the oven to roast until the skins start to open and peel away, about 20 minutes. Remove from the oven, peel and slice, and set aside.

To prepare the capers, pour 2 teaspoons of the olive oil into a frying pan and set over a medium heat. Add the capers and fry until crispy. Remove from the heat and set aside on paper towel.

To make the salsa verde, process the coriander, parsley, dill, garlic and olive oil in a food processor until smooth. Set aside.

For the reduction, pour the olive oil into a frying pan and set over a medium heat. Add the shallots and cook until translucent, about 3–4 minutes. Add the anchovy fillets and cook until browned, another 2–3 minutes. Add the tomatoes and stir to combine. Add the vinegar and stir to deglaze the pan. Remove from the heat and set aside.

For the tuna, pour 2 tablespoons of olive oil in a frying pan over a medium–high heat. Add the tuna and sear until golden, about 1 minute on both sides. Remove from the frying pan, season with sea salt and freshly ground black pepper and set aside to rest.

To serve, thinly slice the rested tuna and place on serving plates. Add the sliced chestnuts, radishes, capers and tomato reduction. Drizzle with salsa verde and garnish with tomato halves, basil leaves, and orange and lemon zest.

Lobster and scallops with herb butter, mushroom panzanella, fennel and orange

This is the dish I cooked for Mum, Dad and Nonna Maria on the finale of MasterChef. It was the first dish of mine they had tried since I left to go on the show. For me, this dish was a different way of looking at Italian food – still the same flavours, just more refined. This dish is all about the layers of flavour and the different textures present.

{ SERVES 4 }

INGREDIENTS

- 1 **lobster**
- 2 **radishes**, thinly sliced on a mandoline
- 200 ml (7 fl oz) **peanut oil**
- 4 **chestnuts**, peeled and thinly sliced on a mandoline
- 200 g (7 oz) **salted butter**
- 1 handful **flat-leaf (Italian) parsley**, roughly chopped
- 1 handful **coriander (cilantro) leaves**, roughly chopped
- **sea salt flakes**
- 60 ml (2 fl oz/¼ cup) **extra-virgin olive oil**
- 1 **French shallot**, finely chopped
- 100 ml (3½ fl oz) **red-wine vinegar**

METHOD

Bring a saucepan of salted water to the boil. Add the lobster and cook, with water simmering, for 8 minutes. Remove from the saucepan and set aside in a bowl of iced water.

Place the radish slices in a separate bowl of iced water and set aside.

Pour the peanut oil into a saucepan and place over a high heat. Bring the oil temperature up to 180°C (350°F). To test if it's ready, drop a breadcrumb into the oil (if it quickly turns golden, then you know the oil is ready). Add the chestnut slices and fry until golden, about 1–2 minutes. Remove from the oil using a slotted spoon and set aside on paper towel.

To make the herb butter, process the butter, parsley and coriander in a food processor until well combined. Season with sea salt and freshly ground black pepper, and set aside.

Heat 1 tablespoon of the oil in a frying pan, add the shallot and fry until caramelised, about 3–4 minutes. Deglaze with red-wine vinegar and cook until jammy. Set aside.

To make the bacon crumb, fry the bacon in a frying pan for a few minutes over a medium–high heat until cooked through. Blitz the cooked bacon in a food processor

- 2 **bacon rashers (slices)**

- 2 slices **sourdough bread**

- 100 g (3½ oz) **oyster mushrooms**, thinly sliced

- 100 g (3½ oz) **shiitake mushrooms**, thinly sliced

- 3 **thyme sprigs**, leaves picked

- 12 **scallops**, roe (coral) removed

- finely grated **orange zest** to garnish

- 1 handful **fennel fronds**

until it has a crumb consistency. Return it to the heated frying pan to crisp up, then drain on some paper towel and set aside.

Pour 2 tablespoons of olive oil in a frying pan and set over a medium heat. Add the sourdough bread and fry on both sides until golden. Remove from the oil, drain on paper towel and tear into pieces. Set aside.

Add another tablespoon of olive oil to the frying pan, add the mushrooms and thyme to the oil, and fry until golden. Remove from the heat, add the fried bread pieces and toss to combine. Season and set aside.

Remove the lobster from the iced water. Remove the meat from the shell and cut into pieces.

Put the herb butter in a frying pan over a medium heat. Add the lobster meat and scallops and cook, basting with the butter, until warmed through, about 1–2 minutes.

To serve, divide the lobster and scallops between serving plates. Add the fried chestnut slices and radish slices. Add the mushrooms and shallot with red-wine vinegar. Sprinkle with the bacon crumb and orange zest and scatter over the fennel fronds, then season with sea salt and freshly ground black pepper.

Lobster and scallops with herb butter, mushroom panzanella, fennel and orange

Bowl of mussels

{ SERVES 4 }

This is one of the simplest yet tastiest dishes in my repertoire. I don't know anyone who's had a whole pot of mussels with crusty bread, and hasn't absolutely loved it. These make a great shared meal to have with friends with a glass of white wine. Don't be shy to double dip – use the mussel shells as a spoon!

INGREDIENTS

- 1 kg (2 lb 3 oz) **mussels**

- 2–3 **roma (plum) tomatoes**

- 2 tablespoons **extra-virgin olive oil**

- 1 **onion**, finely diced

- 2 **garlic cloves**, finely chopped

- 5 **saffron threads** (optional)

- 125 ml (4 fl oz/½ cup) **white wine**

- **sea salt flakes**

- **flat-leaf (Italian) parsley**, roughly chopped, to garnish

- 4 slices **Ciabatta bread** (page 156)

METHOD

To clean the mussels, scrub them with a scourer and pull off the beard of each mussel. Set aside.

To prepare the tomatoes, boil the kettle and pour the boiling water into a heatproof bowl. Score a cross in the base of each tomato and put them in the bowl of hot water. Leave the tomatoes in the bowl until the skins start to peel away, about 30 seconds. Remove the tomatoes from the bowl and peel away the skin, then slice and finely dice.

Pour the olive oil into a large saucepan and set over a medium heat. Add the onion and garlic, and cook until soft, about 3–5 minutes. Add the diced tomatoes and saffron threads (if using) and cook for 5 minutes. Deglaze the pan with the white wine, season with sea salt and freshly ground black pepper, and simmer away for another few minutes.

Add the mussels to the pan, put the lid on and leave to cook for 5–7 minutes. By now all the mussels should have opened. (Discard any mussels that have not opened.)

Transfer the mussels and cooking liquid to a large bowl, sprinkle with parsley and serve with the ciabatta.

Salt-baked snapper

{ SERVES 4 }

This is a recipe that Marco Pierre White taught me. It's a dish that respects and highlights the beauty of the snapper alone, something he feels very strongly about. I love cooking fish like this. The salt crust protects the flesh and allows the fish to be evenly cooked. It's such a simple yet beautiful recipe.

INGREDIENTS

- 1 kg (2 lb 3 oz) **snapper**, whole with scales left on
- 1 kg (2 lb 3 oz) **sea salt**
- **lemon wedges** to serve

METHOD

Preheat the oven to 270°C (520°F).

This recipe requires the scales to be left on the fish. Ask your fishmonger to prepare a snapper, leaving the scales on, so the flesh is protected and it's easy to peel away once cooked.

For the snapper, you need to make a salt covering. To do this, mix 100 ml (3½ fl oz) of water and the salt together. Place half of the salt mixture on the bottom of a baking tray, place the snapper on top and then cover it with the rest of the salt mixture. Make sure the salt layer is thicker at the tail end – you don't want to overcook the tail, as it is much thinner than the upper body.

Press the salt down to pack it firm, and bake in the oven for about 25 minutes.

Once cooked, peel back the salt layer and serve the snapper with your choice of accompaniments, or just with a squeeze of lemon juice. A fennel and orange salad (page 84) would be stunning with this recipe.

CHAPTER FOUR

the land

This is a collection of recipes that are especially wonderful eaten in winter; from the slow-roasted, crispy pork belly to the most melt-in-your-mouth osso bucco. I have incorporated all of my favourites here – chestnuts, artichokes and mushrooms – all with beautiful, delicate flavours to complement the heartiness of each dish.

Roast pork belly

{ SERVES 6 }

Roast pork has always been a favourite in our family. Nonna Rosa would always make roast pork with apple sauce – it was simple yet faultless. Everyone would fight over the pork crackling at the end, and this still happens to this day. This recipe is one of Mum's favourite things to make when guests come over. It just melts in your mouth like butter!

INGREDIENTS

- 2 kg (4 lb 6 oz) **pork belly**, skin left on and scored
- **extra-virgin olive oil**
- **sea salt flakes**
- 20 g (¾ oz/½ bunch) **sage**
- 2 **rosemary sprigs**
- 5 **garlic cloves**, smashed

METHOD

Preheat the oven to 190°C (370°F).

Rub the pork belly with a little olive oil, some sea salt and freshly ground black pepper, with more salt on the skin as it helps it to crisp up.

Place the pork belly in a roasting tin with the sage, rosemary and smashed garlic cloves, even squashing some garlic into the slits on the belly.

Roast for 2½ hours. To crisp up the skin even further, change the oven setting to grill or turn the oven up to 200°C (390°F) and cook the pork for a further 5–10 minutes. Another option is to simply carve off the skin and place in a 200°C (390°F) oven for 10–15 minutes.

Remove the pork belly from the oven and rest for about 10 minutes before serving.

NOTE: THIS ROAST GOES PERFECTLY WITH THE HEIRLOOM CARROTS (PAGE 58), ROAST POTATOES AND A FRESH ORANGE AND FENNEL SALAD (PAGE 84).

Quail with artichokes, mushroom panzanella and red wine jus

{ SERVES 4 }

I created this dish using only ingredients that I love: artichokes, quail, mushrooms, pancetta, and crunchy bread to soak up all the sauce. It brought back memories of having roast quail at Nonna's, digging into crunchy bread straight from the oven, and picking mushrooms in the hills when I was living in Italy. This is a dish that showcases the natural beauty of each ingredient.

INGREDIENTS

JUS

- 1 tablespoon **extra-virgin olive oil**
- 4 × 190 g (6½ oz) **quails**, legs and breasts removed, bones chopped
- 2 **carrots**, roughly chopped
- 2 **onions**, roughly chopped
- 1 **leek**, white part only, roughly chopped
- 6 **sage leaves**, sliced
- 250 ml (8½ fl oz/1 cup) **shiraz wine**
- 30 g (1 oz) **salted butter**, cubed

ARTICHOKES

- juice of 1 **lemon**
- 2 **globe artichokes**
- 1 tablespoon **extra-virgin olive oil**
- 6 **thyme sprigs**
- 420 g (15 oz) **Jerusalem artichokes**
- 50 g (1¾ oz) **salted butter**
- 2 tablespoons **cream**
- **canola oil** for deep-frying

METHOD

Preheat the oven to 200°C (390°F).

To make the jus, place the olive oil in a large frying pan and set over a high heat. Add the quail bones, carrots, onions, leek and sage, and cook for 8–10 minutes, stirring occasionally until caramelised. Add the shiraz and cook for 2 minutes. Add 1 litre (34 fl oz/4 cups) of water, bring to the boil, then reduce to a low–medium heat and simmer for 45 minutes to 1 hour, or until reduced to 80 ml (2½ fl oz/⅓ cup). Strain into a clean saucepan and set aside.

Meanwhile, to prepare the globe artichokes, squeeze the lemon juice into a large bowl of water. Peel the globe artichokes, cut into quarters and remove the choke. Store these in the lemon water to stop the cut artichokes turning brown. Drain, pat dry and place on a baking tray (reserve the lemon water). Drizzle with the olive oil, add the thyme and place in the oven to roast until tender, about 20 minutes. Remove from the oven and set aside.

Peel the Jerusalem artichokes. Use a mandoline to thinly slice 2 artichokes and set aside in the lemon water. Grate the remaining artichokes. Heat the butter in a saucepan over a medium heat. Add the grated artichoke and cook until tender, about 5 minutes. Remove from the heat and transfer to a blender. Add the cream and purée until smooth. Season and pass through a sieve. Set aside, keeping warm.

To prepare the mushrooms, add the butter to a frying pan over a medium heat. Add the mushrooms and sage, and sauté until brown. Remove from the heat, cover and set aside, keeping warm.

MUSHROOMS

- 40 g (1½ oz) **salted butter**
- 200 g (7 oz) **portobello mushrooms**, half thickly sliced, half cut into quarters
- 60 g (2 oz) **oyster mushrooms**, sliced
- 100 g (3½ oz) **enoki mushrooms**
- 4 **sage leaves**, sliced

CARAMELISED ONION

- 1 tablespoon **extra-virgin olive oil**
- 1 **onion**, finely chopped
- 2 **garlic cloves**, thinly sliced
- 250 ml (8½ fl oz/1 cup) **red-wine vinegar**

- 4 slices **baguette**
- 4 slices **pancetta**
- zest of 1 **orange** to garnish

For the caramelised onion, add the olive oil to the frying pan and set over a medium heat. Add the onion and cook until caramelised. Add the garlic and vinegar and cook until thickened and reduced, about 5–6 minutes. Set aside.

Place a chargrill pan over a high heat. Once hot, add the baguette slices and cook each side until char lines appear and the bread is toasted. Remove and set aside. Place the pancetta on the hot chargrill pan and fry until crisp. Remove from the heat and set aside.

Drizzle the quail legs and breasts with a little olive oil and season to ensure all the quail is coated evenly. Heat a frying pan over a medium–high heat. Add the quail, skin side down, and fry until the skin is brown, about 3 minutes. Turn and fry until the quail is cooked through, about another 30 seconds. Remove from the pan and cover to rest and keep warm.

Pour canola oil into a small saucepan until it's approximately one-third full, set it over a high heat and bring the oil temperature up to 180°C (360°F). To test if it's ready, drop a breadcrumb into the oil – if it quickly turns golden, the oil is ready. Drain the Jerusalem artichoke slices and pat dry with paper towel. Add to the hot canola oil and fry in batches until golden and crisp. Remove from the oil and drain on paper towel.

To finish the jus, reheat it over a medium–high heat. Whisk in the cubes of butter, a piece at a time. Season with salt and pepper to taste.

To serve, divide the artichoke purée between plates. Top with quail pieces, mushrooms, caramelised onion, pancetta, roasted globe artichoke and Jerusalem artichoke chips. Sprinkle with orange zest. Serve with the toast and jus.

Quail with artichokes, mushroom panzanella and red wine jus

Pollo alla birra skewers

Chicken with beer

{ SERVES 4 }

For as long as I can remember, Mum has made this dish, but slow-cooked it and served it with a creamy polenta. I decided to create my own take on it by reducing the sauce to get a sticky marinade for the chicken skewers. Serve with polenta chips (page 14) and it makes a great bar-style snack.

INGREDIENTS

- 8 × 150 g (5½ oz) **boneless, skinless chicken thighs**
- 60 ml (2 fl oz/¼ cup) **extra-virgin olive oil**
- 2 **onions**, finely diced
- 2 **garlic cloves**, finely chopped
- 40 g (1½ oz/1 bunch) **sage**, chopped
- 375 ml (12½ fl oz/1½ cups) **pale ale**
- squeeze of **lemon juice**
- 2 tablespoons **brown sugar**

METHOD

Cut the chicken thigh fillets into 2 cm (¾ in) cubes, and line them up on 16 skewers.

Heat 2 tablespoons of the olive oil in a saucepan. Add the onion, garlic and sage, season with salt and pepper, then cook over a low–medium heat until they are lightly caramelised, about 5 minutes.

Pour in the beer to deglaze the pan, and add a squeeze of lemon juice. Slowly reduce the mix to create a sticky sauce. Cook off over a low heat for another 5 minutes, then add the sugar and cook for a further 10 minutes, or until it has reduced by half.

Meanwhile, as the sauce is reducing, heat a chargrill pan over a high heat. Coat the chicken skewers in the remaining oil and season. Cook the chicken on the pan for 3 minutes on each side, or until cooked through.

Add the skewers to the pan with the sauce, give them a quick toss, then plate the skewers up and pour the remaining sauce over the top.

Serve immediately.

Chicken involtino, artichokes, polenta and caponata

{ SERVES 4 }

This was my top 50 dish that got me into MasterChef. I decided to cook this as it showcased my heritage: the polenta is a northern dish, where my Nonno comes from; the caponata is a southern dish, where my Nonna comes from; and the rolled chicken is for my mum, who was first inspired by a street stall selling polenta with stuffed rolled turkey in Tuscany when we lived there. This is a dish dedicated to my beautiful family.

INGREDIENTS

CHICKEN INVOLTINO

- 4 **globe artichokes**
- 4 × 350 g (12½ oz) **chicken leg quarters**, deboned and skin removed
- 6 **rosemary sprigs**, finely chopped
- 6 **sage leaves**, finely chopped
- 50 g (1¾ oz) **Taleggio cheese**, grated
- 16 thin slices **pancetta**, about 150 g (5½ oz)
- 2 tablespoons **olive oil**
- 3 **garlic cloves**, finely chopped
- 4 **bay leaves**
- **basil leaves** to garnish

POLENTA

- 75 g (2¾ oz/½ cup) **polenta**
- 60 ml (2 fl oz/¼ cup) **warm milk**
- 50 g (1¾ oz/½ cup) grated **Parmigiano Reggiano**
- 25 g (1 oz) **salted butter**

- **Caponata** (page 168)

METHOD

Preheat the oven to 200°C (390°F).

Bring a saucepan of water to the boil over a high heat. Clean the artichokes and cut the hearts into quarters, discarding the chokes. Add the artichoke hearts to the boiling water and cook until tender, about 3 minutes. Remove them from the pan and set aside in a bowl of cold water to stop further cooking.

Lay the chicken out flat, flattening each thigh slightly so each piece of chicken is all one thickness. This will ensure equal cooking time. Sprinkle each piece of chicken with 1 teaspoon each of the rosemary and sage, reserving the remaining herbs. Scatter over the Taleggio cheese and season with salt and pepper. Add the cooked artichoke hearts and roll up each piece of chicken. Wrap each chicken roll with 4 slices of pancetta. Tie securely with cooking string.

Add the olive oil to an ovenproof frying pan and place over a high heat. Add the rolled-up chicken and fry until brown on all sides, about 5 minutes. Sprinkle with the remaining rosemary and sage, the garlic and bay leaves, and transfer to the oven. Cook for about 25–30 minutes, or until cooked through. Remove from the oven and set aside to rest.

To make the polenta, put it in a small saucepan with 250 ml (8½ fl oz/1 cup) of water over a medium heat. Stir until combined, then add 250 ml (8½ fl oz/1 cup) of boiling water. Stir every few minutes until the polenta has absorbed all the water and the polenta is soft, about 30 minutes. Add the milk, Parmigiano and butter, and stir until smooth. Remove from the heat, season with salt and pepper to taste, and set aside.

Meanwhile, make the caponata and set aside.

Remove the string from the chicken pieces and slice the chicken. To serve, spread a large spoonful of polenta over each plate, spoon on some caponata sauce and top with the sliced chicken. Garnish with some basil leaves.

Quail, pine mushrooms, chestnuts and polenta

{ SERVES 6 }

This dish takes me back to my two years spent living in La Rocca, a small town in Tuscany. When I created the dish, I was inspired by the Bosco (the forest) near La Rocca, where we would go hunting for mushrooms and chestnuts. I wanted to showcase the story behind this dish, from foraging and hunting for your ingredients, to going home and creating a delicious meal using the freshest of produce.

INGREDIENTS

- 6 **quail**
- 2 tablespoons **extra-virgin olive oil**, plus extra for drizzling
- 1 **carrot**, roughly chopped
- 1 **leek**, white part only, roughly chopped
- 1 **onion**, roughly chopped
- 2 **garlic cloves**, 1 crushed and 1 sliced
- 200 ml (7 fl oz) **sherry**
- 1 litre (34 fl oz/4 cups) **chicken stock**
- 450 g (1 lb) **chestnuts**, scored
- 500 ml (17 fl oz/2 cups) **milk**
- 15 g (½ oz) **salted butter**
- 1½ tablespoons **polenta**
- **sea salt flakes**
- 4 slices **prosciutto**, about 120 g (4½ oz)
- 160 g (5½ oz) **pine mushrooms**, sliced
- 3 **thyme sprigs**, leaves picked
- **wood sorrel** to garnish
- **micro herbs** to garnish

METHOD

Take the breasts and legs off the quail (reserving the carcasses) and place on a baking tray lined with baking paper. Set aside.

Pour 1 tablespoon of the olive oil into a saucepan over a high heat. Add the reserved quail carcasses and fry until browned. Add the carrot, leek, onion and crushed garlic, and continue to cook until brown, about 5–7 minutes. Add the sherry and deglaze the pan. Add the stock and 125 ml (4 fl oz/½ cup) of water, and allow to boil until reduced by half. Remove from the heat, strain, return to the heat and allow to simmer until thickened and reduced. Set aside, keeping warm.

Meanwhile, place the chestnuts on a plate in a single layer in a microwave and cook on high for approximately 2–3 minutes until the skins have opened up. Remove from the microwave, peel and place in a saucepan over a medium heat. Add the milk and butter and bring to the boil. Cover, reduce the heat to low and allow to simmer gently until softened, about 40 minutes.

Transfer the chestnuts and most of the milk to a food processor and pulse to a smooth purée. Add a little more milk if required. Set aside, keeping warm.

Mix the polenta and 185 ml (6 fl oz) of water in a saucepan and cook over a medium heat. Bring to the boil, reduce the heat, and allow to simmer for about 20 minutes until soft. Remove from the heat.

Set a lightly greased crêpe pan over a medium heat. Divide the cooked polenta into six portions. Place one portion in the pan and, using a wet knife or small spatula, spread thinly over the pan. Allow to cook, turning, until crispy on both sides, about 7–8 minutes. Remove from the pan, season with sea salt and freshly ground black pepper and set aside, keeping warm. Repeat with the remaining polenta.

Drizzle the quail breasts and legs with olive oil. Place a chargrill pan over a high heat, add the quail, skin side down and fry until char lines appear, about 2 minutes. Turn and fry until cooked through, about another 1–2 minutes. Remove from the chargrill pan and set aside to rest.

Place a frying pan over a medium heat. Once hot, add the prosciutto slices and cook until crisp, about 5 minutes. Remove them from the frying pan, drain on paper towel, then place them in a food processor and pulse to a crumb. Set aside.

Meanwhile, place 1 tablespoon of olive oil in the frying pan and increase the heat to high. Add the pine mushrooms, the sliced garlic and the thyme, and cook until browned, about 3 minutes. Season and set aside.

To serve, place some chestnut purée on each plate. Add the charred quail breasts and legs, a polenta crisp and some mushrooms. Drizzle with the sauce and sprinkle with prosciutto crumbs. Garnish with wood sorrel and micro herbs, and season with salt and pepper.

NOTE: WOOD SORREL SHOULD BE AVAILABLE FROM MOST GOOD FRUIT SHOPS. YOU CAN ALWAYS ASK FOR IT. FOR THIS MEAL IT'S NOT JUST AN ATTRACTIVE GARNISH – IT BRINGS A WELCOME ACIDITY TO THE WHOLE DISH.

Quail, pine mushrooms, chestnuts and polenta

Mum's osso bucco

{ SERVES 4 }

Most osso bucco recipes are made with a rich tomato sauce, but Mum's version is lovely and light and not as rich as some tomato-based recipes. Packed with flavour, it's a perfect winter warmer that you can leave to simmer for hours.

INGREDIENTS

- 60 ml (2 fl oz/¼ cup) **extra-virgin olive oil**

- **plain (all-purpose) flour** for dusting

- 4 pieces **osso bucco**, about 200–250 g (7–9 oz) per piece

- **sea salt flakes**

- 1 **onion**, finely diced

- 2 **garlic cloves**, thinly sliced

- 3–4 **anchovy fillets**, chopped

- 2 tablespoons **capers**, rinsed, squeezed dry and chopped

- 1 large handful **sage**, chopped

- 2 **rosemary sprigs**, chopped

- 2 handfuls **flat-leaf (Italian) parsley**, finely chopped

- 2 **bay leaves**

- finely grated zest of ½ **lemon**

- juice of 1 **lemon**

- 125 ml (4 fl oz/½ cup) **white wine**

- 250 ml (8½ fl oz/1 cup) **veal** or **chicken stock**

METHOD

Preheat the oven to 180°C (360°F).

Pour half the olive oil into a large ovenproof frying pan and set it on the stove top over a medium–high heat.

Flour the osso bucco and season with sea salt and freshly ground black pepper. Brown the meat, about 3 minutes on both sides, then remove from the frying pan and set aside.

Add the remaining oil to the same frying pan. Cook the onion, garlic and anchovies until soft and translucent, about 3–4 minutes. Add the capers, herbs and lemon zest, and cook for a few minutes.

Deglaze the pan with the lemon juice and white wine, then pour in the stock. Once the sauce starts to bubble, return the osso bucco to the pan. Cover with a lid and place in the preheated oven for 1½–2 hours, or until the meat is tender and falling off the bone.

Serve with polenta (see page 107).

NOTE: CHECK THE OSSO BUCCO FREQUENTLY WHILE IN THE OVEN. IF IT BECOMES A LITTLE DRY, ADD MORE STOCK AS NEEDED.

Sausage, porcini and fennel seed ragu pappardelle

{ SERVES 4 }

Pork, porcini mushrooms and fennel is such a complex combination. This dish is earthy and fresh yet rich, and goes wonderfully well with fresh pappardelle.

INGREDIENTS

- ½ cup **dried porcini mushrooms**
- 3 tablespoons **extra-virgin olive oil**
- 2 **onions**, finely diced
- 2 **garlic cloves**, finely chopped
- 1 long **red chilli**, finely diced
- 400 g (14 oz) **Italian pork sausages**, skin removed and meat broken up
- 1 tablespoon **fennel seeds**
- 125 ml (4 fl oz/½ cup) **white wine**
- **sea salt flakes**
- 500 g (1 lb 2 oz) **fresh pappardelle pasta**
- **Parmigiano Reggiano** to serve

METHOD

Boil the kettle and pour the boiling water into a heatproof bowl with the dried porcini mushrooms to soak for about 10 minutes until they are soft. Drain but reserve the liquid as it has a beautiful porcini mushroom flavour. Roughly chop the mushrooms.

Pour the olive oil into a large saucepan and set over a medium heat. Add the onions, garlic and chilli, and sauté for a few minutes until the onions start to lightly colour.

Add the porcini, broken-up sausage meat and fennel seeds to the onion mixture. Cook for a few minutes until the sausage meat has just cooked through.

Add a little of the porcini water, reduce that by half, and then add the white wine. Cook the wine off and simmer the sauce. Season with sea salt and freshly ground black pepper.

Meanwhile, cook the pasta in boiling salted water until *al dente*, about 3–4 minutes. Strain the pasta and toss through the sauce.

Grate some Parmigiano on top and crack some fresh pepper. Enjoy warm!

Slow-roasted boneless pork loin stuffed with chestnuts and cranberries

{ SERVES 6 }

This is another slow-roasted, mouth-watering roast pork dish that brings back the fondest memories of my two years spent in Tuscany. When chestnuts came into season and were in abundance, we would eat them almost every night, just roasted over the fire after dinner. They provide such a crunchy and creamy texture to this dish. I have a slight addiction to chestnuts, so anywhere I can use them I do. This is my take on Italy's most famous roast, Porchetta.

INGREDIENTS

- 50 g (1¾ oz) **dried cranberries**
- 2 kg (4 lb 6 oz) **boneless pork loin**, plus extra skin (see note below)
- 100 g (3½ oz) **chestnuts**
- 2 tablespoons **extra-virgin olive oil**, plus extra for rubbing into the skin
- 1 **onion**, finely diced
- 1 **garlic clove**, finely chopped
- **sea salt flakes**
- 100 g (3½ oz/1 cup) **dry breadcrumbs**
- finely grated zest of 1 **orange**

METHOD

Preheat the oven to 220°C (430°F).

Boil the kettle and pour the boiling water into a heatproof bowl with the dried cranberries to soak for about 10 minutes until they are soft. Drain and set aside.

Lay the pork loin out flat and pat dry with paper towel to remove any moisture.

Score each chestnut with a small sharp knife, place on a baking tray and roast in the oven for about 20 minutes, or until the skins have opened up.

Remove from the oven, peel back both layers of skin (the harder shell and the brown thin layer of skin), roughly chop the chestnuts and set aside.

Reduce the oven temperature to 160°C (320°F).

To make the stuffing, heat the olive oil in a medium frying pan. Add the onion and garlic and sauté for 3 minutes, or until a light golden colour. Add the rehydrated cranberries, season with sea salt and freshly ground black pepper, and then add the breadcrumbs. Stir for a minute or so to lightly toast the breadcrumbs, then remove from the heat. Add the chestnuts and the orange zest, and stir to combine.

Press the filling onto the laid-out pork loin and roll up the loin, securing it with cooking string to ensure it doesn't come undone while cooking.

Once you have tied up the loin, rub the outside with olive oil and season well. Place in a roasting tin and cook in the oven for 2–2½ hours.

Change the oven setting to grill or increase to 220°C (430°F) and crisp up the skin for 5–10 minutes, continuously rolling the loin over so all the skin becomes crisp.

Rest for 10 minutes on a board, then carve up and serve.

NOTE: EXTRA SKIN IS NEEDED SO THE PORK LOIN IS EASIER TO ROLL UP TO KEEP THE STUFFING SECURE. YOUR LOCAL BUTCHER WILL DO THIS FOR YOU IF YOU ASK.

Sausage, porcini and fennel seed ragu pappardelle

Slow-roasted boneless pork loin stuffed with chestnuts and cranberries

sweets

The most traditional Italian desserts are my favourite
sweets of all time. Tiramisu, biscotti, panna cotta,
crostoli, cannoli ... and the list goes on. These small
pieces of heaven are perfect to finish off your Italian
feast. The trick is making sure these delicious
concoctions of cream, sugar and chocolate aren't
all snapped up by dinnertime.

Zia Dora's famous tiramisu

{ SERVES 6–8 }

My Zia Dora's famous tiramisu recipe is my absolute favourite dessert. I love the creaminess and lightness, and the combination of chocolate and coffee. It has been in my family for generations. Zia Dora gave it to my mum on her honeymoon in Italy, who then passed it down to me.

INGREDIENTS

- 3 **eggs**, separated
- 3 tablespoons **caster (superfine) sugar**
- 500 g (1 lb 2 oz) **mascarpone**
- 500 ml (17 fl oz/2 cups) **espresso coffee**, cooled
- 60 ml (2 fl oz/¼ cup) **dark rum** or **marsala**
- **dark chocolate**, grated for each layer
- 500 g (1 lb 2 oz) **savoiardi (lady fingers) biscuits** (1 large packet)

METHOD

Beat the egg yolks and half the sugar in a bowl for 10–15 minutes until thick and fluffy, and tripled in size. Add the mascarpone and beat until it is fully incorporated.

In a separate bowl, beat the egg whites until stiff peaks form, add the remaining sugar and keep whisking until the sugar has dissolved.

Fold the egg whites into the mascarpone mixture.

In another bowl, mix the coffee and rum/marsala. Dip the biscuits in the coffee and rum mixture.

Arrange a layer of biscuits in the base of a 1.5 litre (51 fl oz/6 cups) capacity bowl or serving dish, then spoon over some of the mascarpone filling, grate some dark chocolate on top, and repeat the layers until your bowl of choice is filled to the top. Finish with the mascarpone mixture. Grate more chocolate over the top and chill in the fridge to set, preferably overnight.

NOTE: SAVOIARDI BISCUITS ARE ALSO KNOWN AS SPONGE FINGER BISCUITS. IF YOU WANT TO HAVE A GO AT COOKING THEM FROM SCRATCH, CHECK OUT MY RECIPE ON PAGE 150.

Chestnut forest
Modern tiramisu

{ SERVES 6 }

This was the dish I created alongside the 'Quail, pine mushrooms, chestnuts and polenta' recipe on MasterChef, matching the dishes through the use of chestnuts. It is meant to replicate a chestnut that has fallen off the tree and onto the forest floor, surrounded by leaves and soil.

INGREDIENTS

PARFAIT

- 65 ml (2¼ fl oz) **milk**
- 2 **eggs**, separated
- 145 g (5 oz) sweetened **chestnut purée**
- 85 g (3 oz) **mascarpone**
- 40 g (1½ oz) **caster (superfine) sugar**
- 65 ml (2¼ fl oz) **cream**
- 2 teaspoons **cacao nibs**

MOUSSE

- 2½ gold-strength **gelatine leaves**, or 2 teaspoons **gelatine powder** dissolved in 60 ml (2 fl oz/¼ cup) boiling water
- 125 ml (4 fl oz/½ cup) **espresso coffee**
- 50 ml (1¾ fl oz) **dark rum**
- 2 **egg whites**
- 65 g (2¼ oz) **sugar**
- 100 ml (3½ fl oz) **cream**

METHOD

Preheat the oven to 170°C (340°F).

To make the parfait, bring the milk to the boil in a small saucepan over a medium heat. Whisk the egg yolks lightly in a bowl. While whisking, slowly add the milk to the egg yolks until combined. Return the mixture to the saucepan and cook over a medium heat, stirring, until the mixture coats the back of the spoon. This will only take a few minutes, so don't turn your back on it!

Remove the saucepan from the heat and transfer the mixture to a food processor. Add the chestnut purée and mascarpone, process until smooth, and set aside.

Beat the egg whites using an electric mixer for approximately 2–3 minutes, gradually adding the sugar until stiff peaks form.

Whisk the cream using an electric mixer until soft peaks form, about 2–4 minutes. You can use a hand-held mixer if you don't have an electric mixer at home.

Add the chestnut purée mixture to the cream and fold to combine. Add the egg whites and fold to combine.

Divide the cacao nibs among six 80 ml (2½ fl oz/⅓ cup) half-dome moulds. Spoon the parfait mixture on top to fill the moulds and set aside in the freezer.

To make the mousse, soak the gelatine leaves in ice-cold water for 5–10 minutes until very soft, and squeeze out any excess water. (If you can't get your hands on gelatine leaves, use gelatine powder dissolved in boiling water.)

Warm the coffee and rum in a small saucepan over a medium heat. Remove the pan from the heat, add the gelatine and stir to combine. Make an ice bath in a large bowl. Strain the coffee–rum mixture into a clean bowl and set aside over the ice bath to cool.

Beat the egg whites using an electric mixer for about 2–3 minutes, gradually adding the sugar until stiff peaks form.

Whisk the cream using an electric mixer until soft peaks form, about 2–4 minutes.

Combine the egg-white mixture, the cooled coffee–rum mixture and the cream, and fold to combine. Set aside in the fridge.

CHOCOLATE CRUMB

- 45 g (1½ oz) **soft brown sugar**
- 35 g (1¼ oz/¼ cup) **plain (all-purpose) flour**
- 30 g (1 oz) **caster (superfine) sugar**
- 30 g (1 oz) **almond meal**
- 25 g (1 oz) **chestnut flour**
- 25 g (1 oz) **cocoa powder**
- 65 g (2¼ oz) **unsalted butter**, melted

GARNISH

- 1 **egg white**
- **fennel fronds**
- 1 teaspoon **caster (superfine) sugar**
- **grape seed oil** for frying
- 50 g (1¾ oz/¼ cup) **wild rice**
- **sea salt flakes**
- 1 teaspoon **cacao nibs**
- **violet flowers**
- **shiso leaves**

NOTE: CHESTNUT PURÉE AND FLOUR CAN BE FOUND AT DELIS AND MEDITERRANEAN FOOD STORES, WHILE HALF-DOME MOULDS ARE SOLD IN HOMEWARE SHOPS. SHISO IS OFTEN AVAILABLE IN ORGANIC OR ASIAN GROCERS, WHILE VIOLET FLOWERS CAN BE FOUND IN GOURMET FOOD STORES.

To make the crumb, combine all the dry ingredients in a bowl. Add the butter and mix well. Spread the mixture on a baking tray lined with baking paper and place in the oven to bake until crunchy, about 20 minutes. Remove from the oven and break into chunks. Set aside.

To crystallise the fennel, place the egg white in a bowl and lightly whisk. Dip the fennel fronds in the egg white to coat. Sprinkle with sugar and set aside on a tray.

To puff the wild rice, pour the grape seed oil into a small saucepan until it is one-third full and place over a high heat until the oil is 180°C (360°F). Drop a small breadcrumb into the hot oil to test if it's ready – if it turns a golden colour straight away, the oil is hot enough. Add the rice and deep-fry until puffed. This should take no more than 10 seconds (otherwise, they'll burn and will be unpleasant to eat). Remove the puffed rice from the oil with a slotted spoon and set aside on paper towel. Lightly sprinkle with sea salt.

To serve, remove the parfait from the freezer and the mousse from the fridge. Scoop some mousse into the bottom of the bowls, sprinkle over the chocolate crumb, puffed rice and some reserved cacao nibs. Tip the parfait into the middle of each bowl. Garnish with violet flowers, shiso leaves and the crystallised fennel fronds.

Nonna's cassatelle

{ MAKES 12 }

This recipe has been handed down in my family for generations. My mum always talks about how her nonna made the best cassatelle ever. She handed down the recipe to my nonna, who handed it to my mother, who handed it to me. It's a bit of a time-consuming recipe, but it's worth it – I love the soft chocolate and almond mixture inside the golden flaky pastry. It's one of Nonna Maria's best desserts!

INGREDIENTS

FILLING

- 300 g (10½ oz) **blanched almonds**
- 230 g (8 oz/1 cup) **caster (superfine) sugar**
- 35 g (1¼ oz/¼ cup) **plain (all-purpose) flour**
- 30 g (1 oz/¼ cup) **cocoa powder**
- finely grated zest of 1 **lemon**
- 1 teaspoon **ground cinnamon**

PASTRY

- 125 g (4½ oz) **caster (superfine) sugar**
- 600 g (1 lb 5 oz/4 cups) **plain (all-purpose) flour**
- 250 g (9 oz) **lard**, at room temperature
- 1 **egg**, lightly beaten

- **icing (confectioners') sugar** for dusting

METHOD

Preheat the oven to 220°C (430°F).

For the filling, scatter the almonds on a baking tray lined with baking paper and roast in the oven until golden, about 5 minutes. Turn the oven off, remove the almonds and grind them in a food processor.

Mix all the dry ingredients together in a saucepan and add 500 ml (17 fl oz/2 cups) of water to the mixture. Combine thoroughly. Cook over a medium heat until it thickens and starts to boil, stirring often until it has a consistency like custard. Allow to cool.

To make the pastry, dissolve the sugar in 200 ml (7 fl oz) of water in a saucepan over a low heat and then cool. Mix the flour, lard, egg and sugar water in a bowl, and knead on a lightly floured surface to form a smooth dough. Cover with plastic wrap and set aside to rest for 30 minutes.

Turn the oven back on and preheat to 220°C (430°F).

Roll out the dough on a floured surface to 5 mm (¼ in) thickness. Cut out circles using a large biscuit (cookie) cutter, 10 cm (4 in) in diameter. Spoon a heaped teaspoon of filling onto each circle. Fold over and crimp the edges with a fork to form a half-moon shape.

Place on a baking tray lined with baking paper and bake for about 10 minutes, or until the pastry is cooked through.

Cool on the tray or on a wire rack, and dust with icing sugar.

Mum's almond bread

{ MAKES 1 LOG, 25 BISCUITS }

Almond bread biscuits are always a winner in our household, and they never last more than a week. In fact, sometimes it's hard to resist eating the whole batch just after they've come out of the oven. They're so delicious!

INGREDIENTS

- 3 **egg whites**, at room temperature
- 90 g (3 oz) **caster (superfine) sugar**
- 90 g (3 oz) **plain (all-purpose) flour**
- 90 g (3 oz) **blanched almonds**
- ½ teaspoon **ground cinnamon**

METHOD

Preheat the oven to 200°C (390°F).

Line a 8 cm × 22 cm (3¼ in × 8¾ in) loaf (bar) tin with baking paper.

Beat the egg whites using an electric mixer until stiff peaks form, then slowly add the caster sugar and continue beating until all the sugar has dissolved. Fold in the flour, almonds and cinnamon.

Pour the mixture into the lined tin and bake for 45–50 minutes, or until golden and firm to touch.

Remove from the tin and cool on a wire rack. When cold, slice the almond log thinly using a serrated knife.

Re-set the oven to 140°C (280°F).

Lay the cut biscuits flat on a baking tray lined with baking paper and bake in the oven for 15 minutes. Turn the biscuits over and bake for a further 15 minutes, or until each biscuit is crisp.

Cool and store in an airtight container in a dry, cool place to ensure they remain crisp.

VARIATIONS: YOU CAN ADD DRIED APRICOTS, PINE NUTS OR ANY OTHER DRIED FRUIT OR NUTS OF YOUR CHOICE. FOR CHRISTMAS-TIME ALMOND BREAD, YOU COULD ADD 90 G (3 OZ) OF CRANBERRIES.

Amaretti biscuits

{ MAKES 20 BISCUITS }

Amaretti biscuits are an all-time favourite of mine. I've grown up eating them every time I went to both my nonnas' houses. They go perfectly with a coffee either in the morning or straight after lunch.

INGREDIENTS

- 4 **egg whites**
- 340 g (12 oz) **caster (superfine) sugar**
- 340 g (12 oz) **almond meal**
- 1 tablespoon **amaretto liqueur**
- 20 **blanched almonds** to top

METHOD

Preheat the oven to 190°C (370°F).

In a large bowl, beat the egg whites using an electric mixer until firm peaks form, about 2–3 minutes. Then slowly add the sugar and beat until all the sugar has dissolved.

Gently fold in the almond meal and amaretto liqueur.

Line two baking trays with baking paper.

Place the mixture into a piping (icing) bag and pipe the mixture into discs, about 2–3 cm (¾–1¼ in) in diameter. Press a blanched almond into the middle of each biscuit.

Bake in the oven for approximately 15 minutes until golden brown. Remove from the oven and cool on a wire rack.

Lemon curd and basil panna cotta with white chocolate noodles

{ SERVES 6 }

The refreshing combination of lemon and basil is everywhere in Italian savoury dishes, but it can also work surprisingly well in a dessert like this one. With the subtle basil flavour of the panna cotta, the sharp tang of the lemon curd, the sweet crunch of the pine nut streusel and the lovely surprise of the white chocolate frozen noodles, this recipe is delicious!

INGREDIENTS

BASIL PANNA COTTA

- 2 **gold-strength gelatine leaves**, or 1½ teaspoons of **gelatine powder** dissolved in 60 ml (2 fl oz/¼ cup) boiling water
- 660 ml (22½ fl oz) **thickened (whipping) cream**
- 40 g (1½ oz) **sugar**
- 100 g (3½ oz/1 bunch) **basil**, leaves picked

LEMON CURD

- 2 **eggs**
- 220 g (8 oz/1 cup) **sugar**
- finely grated zest of 1 **lemon**
- 80 ml (2½ fl oz/⅓ cup) **lemon juice**
- 125 g (4½ oz) **unsalted butter**, cubed

METHOD

Preheat the oven to 190°C (370°F).

To make the panna cotta, soften the gelatine leaves in ice-cold water. Once soft, squeeze off the excess water. (If you can't get your hands on gelatine leaves, use gelatine powder dissolved in boiling water.)

In a saucepan, bring the cream and sugar to a light boil over a medium heat. Remove from the heat, add the basil and leave to infuse for 10–15 minutes, depending on how strong you want the basil flavour.

Add the gelatine and stir through until melted, then pass the liquid through a sieve. Pour the mixture into six 150 ml (5 fl oz) lightly greased dariole moulds. Put in the fridge for 4 hours to set.

For the lemon curd, whisk the eggs and sugar in a heatproof bowl over a saucepan of simmering water until they are light and fluffy, about 5 minutes. During this process, make sure the bowl does not touch the water. Add the lemon zest and juice and keep whisking for another 10 minutes. The mixture will thicken up a lot. Add the butter, one cube at a time, and continue to whisk until well incorporated. Put the mixture in a piping (icing) bag in the fridge until needed for plating.

PINE NUT STREUSEL

- 50 g (1¾ oz/⅓ cup) **pine nuts**
- 20 g (¾ oz) **soft brown sugar**
- 35 g (1¼ oz) **caster (superfine) sugar**
- 20 g (¾ oz) **unsalted butter**, melted

FROZEN WHITE CHOCOLATE NOODLES

- 1 × 200 g (7 oz) packet **white cooking chocolate**
- bowl of **ice-cold water**

- small **basil leaves** to garnish

For the streusel, blitz the pine nuts with the sugars and butter in a food processor to form a crumb. Bake for 5 minutes on a baking tray lined with baking paper. Set aside.

For the frozen white chocolate noodles, melt the chocolate, either in the microwave or over a double boiler, and pour it into a piping (icing) bag with a 4–5 mm (¼ in) nozzle.

Pipe the melted chocolate into the ice-cold water. As the chocolate falls to the bottom of the bowl, it will harden. Remove it and refrigerate until needed.

Transfer the panna cotta from the moulds onto serving plates, pipe some curd on the plates, sprinkle with the pine nut streusel, and top with the frozen chocolate noodles and basil leaves.

Lemon curd and basil panna cotta with white chocolate noodles

Natalie's mocha mud cakes

{ MAKES 24 }

This recipe is dedicated to my best friend, my sister Natalie. Thank you for showing me how to make these rich chocolate mud cakes with a beautiful velvety coffee frosting. They are absolute perfection!

INGREDIENTS

- 185 g (6½ oz) **dark cooking chocolate**, roughly chopped
- 125 g (4½ oz) **unsalted butter**, chopped
- 60 g (2 oz/⅓ cup lightly packed) **soft brown sugar**
- 2 teaspoons **instant coffee**
- 1 **egg**, beaten
- 75 g (2¾ oz/½ cup) **plain (all-purpose) flour**
- 2 tablespoons **self-raising flour**
- **coffee beans** to decorate

COFFEE BUTTER CREAM

- 25 g (1 oz) **unsalted butter**
- 200 g (7 oz) **icing (confectioners') sugar**, sifted
- 2 tablespoons **espresso coffee**
- 1 tablespoon **milk**
- few drops **natural vanilla extract**

METHOD

Preheat the oven to 170°C (340°F).

Combine the chocolate, butter, brown sugar, 80 ml (2½ fl oz/⅓ cup) of water and the instant coffee in a medium saucepan over a low heat. Stir until the chocolate has melted, about 5 minutes.

Once the chocolate has melted, cool slightly and then pour the mixture into a bowl. Add the egg, then slowly sift in the flours and incorporate.

Grease a 24-hole mini-muffin pan and then divide the mixture equally among the 24 muffin pan holes.

Bake the muffins for 15 minutes or until cooked through. Let them rest in the pan for a further 10 minutes before removing them and cooling on a wire rack.

To make the coffee butter cream, beat the butter using an electric mixer until soft and white coloured, then slowly add the icing sugar.

Add the coffee, milk and vanilla, and beat until all the ingredients are incorporated.

Spoon the icing into a piping (icing) bag and pipe the icing onto the now cooled mini muffins. Decorate with whole coffee beans.

Profiteroles with orange cinnamon ricotta

Profiteroles are always a crowd pleaser at family events. Instead of using the traditional custard I like to put my own spin on these by using orange, cinnamon and ricotta, a traditional Sicilian combination ... It really is to die for!

{ MAKES 24 }

INGREDIENTS

PROFITEROLES

- 75 g (2¾ oz) **unsalted butter**, diced
- 150 g (5½ oz/1 cup) **plain (all-purpose) flour**, sifted
- 4 **eggs**
- melted **dark cooking chocolate** for dunking

ORANGE CINNAMON RICOTTA FILLING

- 500 g (1 lb 2 oz/2 cups) **fresh ricotta**
- 75 g (2¾ oz/½ cup) finely chopped **dark chocolate**
- 80 g (2¾ oz/⅓ cup) **caster (superfine) sugar**
- finely grated zest of 4 **oranges**
- 2 teaspoons **ground cinnamon**

METHOD

Preheat the oven to 260°C (500°F).

In a small saucepan, place 250 ml (8½ fl oz/1 cup) of water and the butter over a low heat and bring to the boil until the butter is melted.

Add the flour and a pinch of salt and, using a wooden spoon, beat the mixture until a ball forms and doesn't stick to the side of the saucepan.

Remove the dough from the heat. Allow the mixture to cool slightly before transferring into the bowl of an electric mixer. Turn on to a low speed, adding the eggs one at a time, but beating well after each addition. The mixture should be thick, glossy and very smooth.

Line two baking trays with baking paper and place dollops of the mixture about 1 teaspoon in size onto the trays, allowing room for spreading.

Bake for 10 minutes, then drop the temperature to 180°C (360°F) and cook for a further 40 minutes until the puffs are golden and firm.

Once the profiteroles have cooked through, make an incision in the base of each one with a knife to release the steam, and place back in the turned-off oven to dry out. This will only take a few minutes.

While the profiteroles are cooling down, make the filling.

Mix the ricotta, chocolate, sugar, orange zest and cinnamon in a bowl until it is all incorporated.

Spoon the filling into a piping (icing) bag and pipe some filling into each profiterole, then dip into the melted chocolate.

Serve immediately, when they are at their best.

Cannoli

{ MAKES 30 SHELLS }

I can't say no to cannoli. They're the one temptation that I simply can't turn down. They're crispy and creamy, and just a mouthful of absolute heaven! They are one of Italy's most popular desserts, so they're often enjoyed at the end of a meal with an espresso coffee. This recipe is a bit time-consuming, and takes a few hours to complete, but I think there's greater satisfaction in making your own cannoli shells than buying them. Cannoli are best enjoyed fresh, when they are nice and crispy.

INGREDIENTS

PASTRY

- 680 g (1½ lb) **plain (all-purpose) flour**
- 160 g (5½ oz/⅔ cup) **lard**, melted (use butter if lard isn't available)
- 125 g (4½ oz/1 cup) **icing (confectioners') sugar**
- 250 ml (8½ fl oz/1 cup) **marsala**
- 4 **egg yolks**
- 3 **eggs**, 1 lightly beaten for egg wash

CUSTARD

- 3 **egg yolks**
- 100 g (3½ oz) **caster (superfine) sugar**
- 100 g (3½ oz) **cornflour (cornstarch)**
- 1 litre (34 fl oz/4 cups) **warm milk**
- 1 **vanilla bean**, halved and seeds scraped

- **canola oil** for deep-frying
- **icing (confectioners') sugar** for dusting

METHOD

For the pastry, mix the flour and lard together in a large mixing bowl, then add all the other ingredients and form the dough. Alternatively (if using butter), combine the flour and butter in a food processor until they resemble breadcrumbs, then add the remaining ingredients to form a dough. Cover with plastic wrap and rest for 1 hour.

Set up a pasta machine, divide the dough into four portions and roll each through the machine, adjusting the settings until the dough is 1 mm thick.

Lay the sheets on a lightly floured surface and cut circle shapes (by hand) to 10 cm (4 in) in diameter. Brush the edges with the beaten egg and wrap over a cannoli mould.

Pour canola oil into a small saucepan until it's one-third full and place over a medium-high heat until the oil is 180°C (360°F). Drop a small piece of dough into the hot oil to test if it's ready – if it turns a golden colour straight away, the oil is hot enough. Deep-fry each cannoli for 30 seconds. Drain on paper towel and remove the moulds.

For the custard, whisk the egg yolks and sugar in a bowl until thick and pale. Add the cornflour and a dash of milk and continue mixing until well combined, then add the remaining milk.

Add the vanilla bean and seeds to the mixture, pour it into a medium saucepan and cook over a low–medium heat, stirring constantly until the mixture thickens and starts to boil, about 5 minutes. Reduce the heat and simmer for a further 5 minutes. Once the custard has cooked, remove the vanilla bean.

Cool the custard. Once cooled, pour into a piping (icing) bag with a 2 cm (¾ in) nozzle and pipe into the cannoli shells. Dust with icing sugar and serve.

NOTE: CANNOLI MOULDS CAN BE BOUGHT FROM HOMEWARE SHOPS.

Crostoli

{ MAKES 40 }

If you've never had crostoli before, then do yourself a favour and try this recipe. It's a bit of an effort to make these, but definitely worth it. They are so addictive once you start to eat them, like crunchy pillows of air – and the best part is getting icing sugar everywhere when you're eating them.

INGREDIENTS

- 300 g (10½ oz/2 cups) **self-raising flour**
- 300 g (10½ oz/2 cups) **plain (all-purpose) flour**
- 250 ml (8½ fl oz/1 cup) **sweet white wine (or dessert wine)**
- 1 large **egg**
- 2 tablespoons **extra-virgin olive oil**
- 2 tablespoons **caster (superfine) sugar**
- finely grated zest of 1 **lemon**
- 1 teaspoon **natural vanilla extract**
- **canola oil** for frying
- **icing (confectioners') sugar** for dusting

METHOD

Mix together the flours, wine, egg, olive oil, caster sugar, lemon zest and vanilla to form a dough. This can be done by hand or in a food processor. Either way, make sure not to overwork the dough, which should be smooth and elastic, and not too firm. Cover and rest at room temperature for 30 minutes.

Divide the dough into six portions and, using a pasta machine, roll out the dough to the Number 6 setting on the machine.

Place the sheets on a lightly floured surface and cut them into 3 cm (1¼ in) strips using a fluted pastry cutter. Cut a slit lengthways along the middle of each strip, finishing 2 cm (¾ in) from each end. Hoop one end through the slit to form a twist.

Heat a deep frying pan approximately one-quarter full with canola oil and set over a medium–high heat until the oil is approximately 180°C (360°F). Drop a small piece of pastry into the oil to test if the oil is ready – if it turns a golden colour straight away, the oil is hot enough. Fry the pastry strips in batches for about 4 minutes per batch, until golden on all sides.

Remove the crostoli with a slotted spoon and place on paper towel to drain off any excess oil, then dust with icing sugar and serve.

Tangy citrus cheesecakes

{ SERVES 6 }

This is one of Dad's favourite desserts. All he ever wants is lime cheesecake.
It's so light and refreshing that I can understand why!

INGREDIENTS

- 125 g (4½ oz) **plain sweet biscuits**, crushed

- 45 g (1½ oz/½ cup) **desiccated coconut**

- 80 g (2¾ oz) **unsalted butter**, melted

- 3 **gold-strength gelatine leaves**, softened in water, or use 2 teaspoons **gelatine powder** dissolved in 60 ml (2 fl oz/¼ cup) boiling water

- 250 g (9 oz/1 cup) **cream cheese**, softened

- 55 g (2 oz/¼ cup) **caster (superfine) sugar**

- 395 g (14 oz) **sweetened condensed milk**

- 125 ml (4 fl oz/½ cup) **thickened (whipping) cream**

- finely grated zest and juice of 2 **lemons** and 2 **limes**

- **strawberries**, halved, to serve

METHOD

Mix the crushed biscuits with the coconut and butter in a bowl. This forms the base of the cheesecake so make sure the crumbs aren't too big. Press the crumb mixture into six 10 cm (4 in) greased, round spring-form cake tins. Refrigerate the cheesecake bases until needed.

Soak the gelatine leaves in ice-cold water for about 5–10 minutes. When ready to use, squeeze out the excess water. (Alternatively, dissolve the gelatine powder in the boiling water.)

Using an electric mixer, beat the cream cheese and sugar until the mixture is smooth with no lumps, then beat in the condensed milk, cream and gelatine. Fold through the lime and lemon zest and juice, and pour into the pre-chilled cheesecake bases. Chill for 3 hours or until set.

Serve the cheesecakes with fresh strawberries.

Chocolate and blood orange panna cotta

{ SERVES 6 }

Panna cotta, meaning cooked cream, is such a lovely traditional Italian dessert, and here I have showcased the beautiful combination of chocolate, orange and hazelnut. Panna cotta is a great dessert to show off with at a dinner party for your friends, and can be made the night before! You don't have to make it as fancy as this one. If you want to simplify it, use this recipe as a base, but add vanilla beans and serve it with fresh berries.

INGREDIENTS

CHOCOLATE PANNA COTTA

- 2 **gold-strength gelatine leaves**, or 1½ teaspoons **gelatine powder** dissolved in 60 ml (2 fl oz/¼ cup) of boiling water
- 660 ml (22½ fl oz) **thickened (whipping) cream**
- 40 g (1½ oz) **caster (superfine) sugar**
- 220 g (8 oz) **milk chocolate**, chopped finely

BLOOD ORANGE JELLY

- 400 ml (13½ fl oz) **blood orange juice**
- 4 **gold-strength gelatine leaves**, or 4 teaspoons **gelatine powder**

BLOOD ORANGE CURD

- 2 **eggs**
- 230 g (8 oz/1 cup) **caster (superfine) sugar**
- finely grated zest of 1 **blood orange**
- 80 ml (2½ fl oz/⅓ cup) **blood orange juice**
- 125 g (4½ oz) **unsalted butter**, cubed

METHOD

For the panna cotta, soak the gelatine leaves in ice-cold water until soft, about 5–10 minutes. When it's time to add to the panna cotta mixture, squeeze the excess water out of the gelatine leaves first. If you're using gelatine powder instead, dissolve the powder in the boiling water.

To make the blood orange jelly, pour the juice into a saucepan and set over a medium heat. Bring to a simmer, remove from the heat, add the gelatine and stir until dissolved. Allow to cool. Pass through a sieve, and pour equal amounts into six 150 ml (5 fl oz) dariole moulds. Set in the fridge on a tray for about 45 minutes. To speed up the process, place in the freezer for 10 minutes until set.

To make the panna cotta, pour the cream and sugar into a saucepan and set over a medium heat. Bring to a simmer, remove from the heat, add the chopped chocolate and whisk until it is all combined. Add the gelatine and stir until dissolved. Strain through a fine sieve and allow to cool slightly. Pour over the already set blood orange jelly, then place back in the fridge to set for about 4 hours. Note: The panna cotta can be made the day before and set overnight.

To make the blood orange curd, set up a double boiler. Add the eggs and sugar and whisk until slightly thickened and creamy. Add the blood orange zest and juice and continue to whisk for about 10–15 minutes until the mixture thickens. Once thickened, add the butter cubes one at a time until glossy and all incorporated. Leave to cool, then refrigerate.

HAZELNUT CRUMB

- 110 g (4 oz/1 cup) **hazelnut meal**
- 75 g (2¾ oz/½ cup) **plain (all-purpose) flour**
- 115 g (4 oz/½ cup) **caster (superfine) sugar**
- 95 g (3¼ oz/½ cup lightly packed) **soft brown sugar**
- 100 g (3½ oz) **unsalted butter**, melted

TO GARNISH

- **strawberries**, halved and whole
- **raspberries**, halved and whole
- **blood orange** segments, membrane removed

Preheat the oven to 220°C (430°F).

For the hazelnut crumb, mix the hazelnut meal, flour, both sugars and the melted butter in a bowl until all combined. Spread on a baking tray lined with baking paper and bake for 20–25 minutes until golden and crunchy. Check the crumb every 10 minutes and turn the mixture over to ensure nothing is burning.

When it's time to serve, transfer the panna cotta from the moulds onto serving plates, add the curd and crumb, and garnish with fresh berries and blood orange segments.

Chocolate and blood orange panna cotta

Savoiardi biscuits

{ MAKES 20-24 }

I came up with this recipe one day when I decided I wanted to make tiramisu from scratch, and didn't want to use packet biscuits. These homemade savoiardi (lady fingers) ended up being a real discovery. They are so delicious, even just by themselves with a cup of coffee.

INGREDIENTS

- 4 **eggs**, separated
- 1 **vanilla bean**, halved and seeds scraped
- 145 g (5 oz/⅔ cup) **caster (superfine) sugar**, plus extra for sprinkling
- 110 g (4 oz/¾ cup) **plain (all-purpose) flour**, sifted
- pinch of **salt**

METHOD

Preheat the oven to 190°C (370°F).

In the bowl of an electric mixer, beat the egg yolks, the vanilla seeds and half of the sugar until thick and pale, about 5–10 minutes.

In another bowl, beat the egg whites until soft peaks form, then slowly add the remaining sugar, beating until all the sugar has dissolved.

Gently fold the egg whites into the egg yolk mixture, and then fold through the flour and salt.

Pour the mixture into a disposable piping (icing) bag. You don't need a nozzle. Just cut the tip off the bag so it is 1 cm (½ in) in diameter, and pipe finger-length shapes onto baking trays lined with baking paper, ensuring there is enough space for the biscuits to grow in the oven.

Bake for 15–20 minutes, or until the biscuits are firm and golden.

Remove from the oven, cool on a wire rack and sprinkle with caster sugar. Store in an airtight container, or use straight away to make tiramisu.

Biscotti

{ MAKES 60 }

In Italian, biscotti means twice cooked. There's nothing more enjoyable than having a crunchy biscotto in the morning with an espresso shot. It's the perfect way to start the day.

INGREDIENTS

- 125 g (4½ oz/1 cup) **blanched slivered almonds**
- 125 g (4½ oz) **unsalted butter**, softened
- 170 g (6 oz/¾ cup) **caster (superfine) sugar**
- 3 **eggs**
- 2 tablespoons **brandy**
- 1 tablespoon finely grated **lemon zest**
- 225 g (8 oz/1½ cups) **plain (all-purpose) flour**, sifted
- 110 g (4 oz/¾ cup) **self-raising flour**, sifted
- 1 tablespoon **aniseeds** (or fennel seeds)

METHOD

Preheat the oven to 200°C (390°F).

Spread the almonds on a baking tray and put them in the oven for approximately 5 minutes, until the almonds are golden brown. Allow to cool.

Using an electric mixer, cream the butter and sugar for approximately 5–8 minutes until light and fluffy, scraping the bowl occasionally.

Add the eggs one at a time, mixing after each one to incorporate fully. Mix in the brandy and lemon zest.

Stir the flours into the butter mixture, then add the almonds and aniseeds and gently combine.

Turn the mixture out onto a lightly floured surface. Knead lightly and divide the mixture into three. Shape and roll into logs, approximately 30 cm (12 in) long.

Place the rolls on a baking tray lined with baking paper. Refrigerate for 1 hour.

Approximately 10 minutes before the rolls are due to come out of the refrigerator, preheat the oven to 180°C (360°F).

Bake the rolls for approximately 20 minutes or until lightly browned. Cool on a wire rack.

Cut the rolls into 1 cm (½ in) slices with a serrated knife.

Spread the biscotti on a baking tray lined with baking paper and bake for about 25–30 minutes, or until dry and crisp, turning them halfway through the cooking time.

Cool and store in a sealed airtight container. They will last for about 1 month.

NOTE: IF YOU CAN'T GET YOUR HANDS ON ANISEEDS, YOU CAN ALWAYS USE FENNEL SEEDS. THEY HAVE A SIMILAR TASTE AND ARE A GOOD SUBSTITUTE.

basics

There's nothing quite like an abundant pantry, overflowing with lovingly prepared staples, ready to use at a moment's notice. This chapter includes the essential basics you'll need to master the art of Italian cuisine, from pasta doughs to marinated vegetables, pickles and sauces. Here are a few of my favourite staples, from my pantry to yours.

Ciabatta bread

{ MAKES 2 LOAVES }

Baking your own bread is such a satisfying activity. Not only are you able to enjoy the fresh flavour and wonderful soft texture of the bread, you also get the chance to savour the delicious aroma that will fill your house and relish the sense of achievement when you serve up a complete meal that's been whipped up from scratch in your own kitchen. Crusty ciabatta bread, toasted as bruschetta the next day, is even better! Mum is always making bread at home, and this recipe is one of her best ones!

INGREDIENTS

- 500 g (1 lb 2 oz/3⅓ cups) **strong flour**
- 1 teaspoon **dried yeast**
- 360 ml (12 fl oz) lukewarm **water**

METHOD

Mix all the ingredients using an electric mixer for approximately 10–12 minutes on a low speed using a dough hook attachment, then for another 10–12 minutes on a medium speed. This step can also be done by hand on a well-floured work surface, but using a mixer gives a much better result.

The dough should be wet and sticky. Transfer the dough to a lightly oiled bowl. Cover with plastic wrap and leave to rest in a warm place for 1 hour.

Divide the dough in half and, using plenty of dusting flour, grasp the ends of the dough and gently stretch into shape. The dough should be about 5–6 cm (2–2½ in) thick.

Carefully place each piece of stretched dough onto a well-floured baking tray. Cover with plastic wrap and leave to rest in a warm place for a further 40 minutes. Ten minutes before the end of the dough's resting time, preheat the oven to 250°C (480°F).

Bake for 25 minutes or until golden and cooked through.

Cool on the baking trays.

NOTE: YOU CAN KNEAD THIS MIXTURE BY HAND IF YOU DON'T HAVE A MIXER WITH A DOUGH HOOK ATTACHMENT. IT'LL TAKE A LOT OF HARD WORK BUT IT CAN BE DONE.

Focaccia

While we were living in Italy, Mum would drive us to the local bakery before school nearly every morning, and I'd always choose the potato focaccia. I just can't resist it! Focaccia is such a versatile flatbread. You can eat it like regular sliced bread, fill it with cheese and salami or a fresh prosciutto – the combinations are endless. This is a great recipe to make with kids, who love getting involved, whether it's mixing the dough, watching it rise, poking the holes, or impatiently waiting for it to cook so it can be eaten warm and fresh, pretty much straight out of the oven!

INGREDIENTS

- 600 g (1 lb 5 oz/4 cups) **00 flour**
- 1 tablespoon **dried yeast**
- 1 teaspoon **salt**
- 500 ml (17 fl oz/2 cups) **warm water**
- 1 tablespoon **extra-virgin olive oil**, plus extra for coating dough
- **sea salt flakes** for sprinkling

METHOD

Mix the dry ingredients together in a large bowl. Add three-quarters of the water and the olive oil, and mix well. Add enough extra water to make a moist, stiff dough. You may not need all of the water.

Gently knead the dough to form a ball. Lightly oil the ball of dough and place in a bowl. Cover with plastic wrap and leave in a warm place to rest and double in size, about 1 hour.

Divide the dough into two, roll out on a lightly floured surface and place on two 15 cm × 30 cm (6 in × 12 in) baking trays lined with baking paper. Rest for another hour, covered with plastic wrap or a tea towel (dish towel).

Preheat the oven to 210°C (410°F).

Push holes into the focaccias with your finger, drizzle with olive oil and season with salt flakes. Bake for 25–30 minutes until golden and cooked through.

Cool on wire racks.

Pizza base

{ MAKES 3–4 PIZZAS OR
1 VERY LARGE PIZZA }

Pizza would have to be one of the best meals invented. I love how versatile you can be with toppings, adding whatever ingredients you have in the fridge and pantry. Growing up, we would have a pizza night most weekends, and I loved being in charge of toppings. Being the foodie in the house, I always wanted extravagant toppings, and the three combinations I've provided for this book are three of my favourites!

Tomato, buffalo mozzarella and basil (page 60)
Potato, caramelised onions and rosemary oil (page 61)
Gorgonzola, prosciutto, rocket and pesto (page 65)

INGREDIENTS

- 600 g (1 lb 5 oz/4 cups) **00 flour**
- 1 tablespoon **dried yeast**
- 1 teaspoon **salt**
- 500 ml (17 fl oz/2 cups) **warm water**
- 1 tablespoon **extra-virgin olive oil**, plus extra for coating dough and hands

METHOD

Mix the dry ingredients together in a large bowl. Add the olive oil and three-quarters of the water, and mix together. Add enough extra water to make a moist, stiff dough.

On a lightly floured surface, gently knead the dough to form a ball. Lightly oil the ball of dough and place in a bowl. Cover with plastic wrap and leave in a warm place to rest and double in size, about 1 hour.

Preheat the oven to 220°C (430°F).

Divide the dough into three or four balls, depending on how big your trays are. Lightly oil your hands and press the dough into greased trays about 2 cm (¾ in) deep.

Top with your favourite toppings.

Cook pizzas for about 15 minutes, or until the bases are crisp.

Pasta dough

{ SERVES 4–6, MAKES ABOUT
1.5 KG (3 LB 5 OZ) FRESH PASTA }

This is a very hands-on recipe. There's a certain pleasure in getting your hands dirty and full of pasta dough, making it quite a fun and relaxing job. I have been making pasta for as long as I can remember. One of my earliest childhood memories is making this recipe with my mum, nonna and sister in the kitchen, all of us having different jobs: kneading the pasta, rolling it through the machine, cutting it and making all different types of shapes. I believe there's no greater satisfaction than seeing the creation of a whole dish from start to finish. Making fresh pasta is one of the most rewarding things you can do in the kitchen.

INGREDIENTS

- 600 g (1 lb 5 oz/4 cups) **00 flour**
- 250 g (9 oz/2 cups) **semolina**
- 4 **eggs**
- 1 tablespoon **extra-virgin olive oil**

METHOD

Mix the flour and semolina together, either in a large mixing bowl or on a clean work surface. Make a well in the centre of the flour mixture and add the eggs, around 190 ml (6½ fl oz/¾ cup) of water, the olive oil and a pinch of salt. Mix until thoroughly combined, either with a fork or using your hands. If the mixture is too dry, add another 60 ml (2 fl oz/¼ cup) of water.

Knead the mixture until you form a soft and smooth dough that is pliable. (If the mixture is too sticky, add a little more flour.)

Shape the dough into a ball, cover with plastic wrap and leave to rest for about 30 minutes.

Divide the pasta dough into six portions and flatten into disc shapes. Dust with semolina.

Pass each pasta disc through a pasta machine, starting on the thickest setting (settings on different machines vary). When passing the pasta through the thickest setting (setting Number 1), you will have to roll it through a few times, folding the pasta in half each time until it comes out as a smooth pasta sheet.

Continue to pass it through only once on each setting until you reach your desired thickness. Your pasta sheets will be thin and smooth once finished. Cut into the desired shapes or leave whole for lasagne.

NOTE: YOU CAN STORE PASTA SHEETS OR ANY PASTA SHAPE IN THE FREEZER, BETWEEN SHEETS OF BAKING PAPER IN A SEALED CONTAINER. IT WILL LAST 3 MONTHS.

Traditional gnocchi

{ SERVES 6-8 }

One of my first memories of making fresh gnocchi was with my late Nonna Rosa in Tuscany at age six. She was one of the most incredible cooks I have ever come across, but for some reason that day there was more flour on the floor and in the cracks of the benches than in the gnocchi itself. My favourite way to have gnocchi is with pesto, but napolitana sauce is also great. Even simple butter and sage is a beautiful combination with gnocchi.

INGREDIENTS

- 1 kg (2 lb 3 oz) **potatoes** (desiree and toolangi delight are the best I've found for gnocchi)
- 300 g (10½ oz/2 cups) **00 flour**, plus extra if needed
- 1 **egg**

METHOD

Peel the potatoes, and chop them into cubes. Put the potatoes in a stockpot of cold salted water and bring to the boil. Cook for a further 15–20 minutes, or until the potatoes are cooked all the way through.

Pass the potatoes through a sieve into a large bowl. Add the flour gradually, along with the egg and a pinch of salt, mixing until well combined. Knead the dough gently on a floured surface.

Cut the dough into smaller portions and roll into long thin sausage shapes. Cut the sausage-shaped rolls into 3 cm (1¼ in) pieces, then roll into balls.

Gently press a fork into the balls to get an indented mark on the gnocchi.

To cook, add the gnocchi to a large saucepan of boiling salted water and cook for 3 minutes, or until they float to the surface. Drain.

NOTE: THE BEST POTATOES TO USE FOR GNOCCHI ARE WHITE-FLESHED FLOURY POTATOES. YELLOW-FLESHED WAXY POTATOES ARE NOT SUITABLE FOR MAKING GNOCCHI AS THEY TURN TO GLUE! AS LONG AS YOU USE A FLOURY POTATO, YOU SHOULD BE ABLE TO ACHIEVE THE PERFECT GNOCCHI.

Traditional gnocchi on the left and Pasta dough on the right

Polenta

Polenta is one of my favourite ingredients, and can be used in lots of different ways. You can have a wet soft polenta as in this recipe, but you can also use it to make cakes, delicious polenta chips or wafers, just to name a few. Soft polenta is such a hearty accompaniment for osso bucco, casserole or caponata. It's a perfect winter warmer!

INGREDIENTS

- 300 g (10½ oz/2 cups) **polenta**
- 1.5 litres (51 fl oz/6 cups) **boiling water**
- **sea salt**
- 50 g (1¾ oz) **salted butter**, chopped
- 125 ml (4 fl oz/½ cup) **milk**

METHOD

Pour 500 ml (17 fl oz/2 cups) of cold water into a large saucepan and add the polenta. Whisk until smooth, then pour in the boiling water. Continue to whisk over a medium heat until the water and polenta has combined, and starts to bubble.

Lower the heat to a simmer, season with sea salt, and cook for approximately 30 minutes, stirring occasionally with a wooden spoon. Add the butter and milk, and stir until the butter has melted and the mixture has combined.

Pour the polenta into a serving dish.

Chicken stock

{ MAKES ABOUT 1.5 LITRES
(51 FL OZ/6 CUPS) }

A good chicken stock is one of the most essential recipes to have. It's a perfect base for beautiful jus and sauces. This is such an easy one, and can be tweaked and changed as you please. You can replace the chicken leg quarters with fish bones, or any other meat bones of your choice.

INGREDIENTS

- 2 **chicken leg quarters**
- 1 **carrot**, roughly chopped
- 1 **celery stalk (leaves included)**, roughly chopped
- 1 **onion**, roughly chopped
- 1 **leek**, white part only, roughly chopped
- 6 **peppercorns**
- 2 **bay leaves**

METHOD

Heat the chicken, carrot, celery, onion, leek, peppercorns and bay leaves in a large saucepan with 2 litres (68 fl oz/8 cups) of water and simmer for a couple of hours to get the maximum flavour.

Strain and return the stock to the stove top over a low heat to keep warm if using in a recipe straight away. Otherwise, this stock can be refrigerated or frozen for future use.

Napolitana
Basic tomato sauce

{ MAKES ABOUT 850 ML (28½ FL OZ) }

I don't think anything can beat a plate of fresh pasta with a simple tomato sauce. It's one of the best comfort meals ever, and is a regular Sunday night dinner in my family. Serve with fresh basil leaves – perfection!

INGREDIENTS

- 2 tablespoons **extra-virgin olive oil**
- 1 **onion**, finely diced
- 1 **garlic clove**, finely chopped
- **sea salt flakes**
- 800 g (1 lb 12 oz) **tinned chopped tomatoes**
- 50 g (1¾ oz/½ bunch) **basil**, leaves picked
- 1 teaspoon **sugar**

METHOD

Heat the olive oil in a saucepan over a medium heat and fry the onions and garlic until lightly caramelised, about 3–5 minutes. Season with sea salt and freshly ground black pepper.

Add the tomatoes and basil, and season again, this time with sugar and sea salt.

Place a lid on the saucepan, and simmer away for 20–25 minutes.

Taste and stir every 10 minutes, adding extra seasoning if needed.

Pesto

{ MAKES ABOUT 250 ML (8½ FL OZ) }

I love a classic pesto, and always have it on hand in the fridge. It's so versatile, and can be used in pasta recipes, for gnocchi, on pizzas or even in salads. There are lots of different ways to make it (without garlic, using cashews instead of pine nuts), but I love my recipe as it's quite traditional. Using Parmigiano Reggiano rather than a basic parmesan gives the sauce a much nuttier flavour and a lovely subtle saltiness.

INGREDIENTS

- 100 g (3½ oz/1 bunch) **basil**, leaves picked
- 40 g (1½ oz/¼ cup) **pine nuts**
- 25 g (1 oz/¼ cup) grated **Parmigiano Reggiano**
- 125 ml (4 fl oz/½ cup) **extra-virgin olive oil**, plus extra for storing
- 1 **garlic clove**, crushed

METHOD

Blitz all the ingredients in a food processor until smooth, scraping down the sides to ensure it is all incorporated. Adjust seasoning if required.

Spoon the pesto into a jar, cover with extra-virgin olive oil and seal with a lid. Refrigerate and use as required. This should last up to a week, if covered in oil and stored in a jar or airtight container.

Caponata

{ MAKES ABOUT 750 G (1 LB 11 OZ) }

Caponata is one of my favourite side dishes. I love serving this with warm winter dishes, especially my chicken involtino. The very traditional Sicilian caponata uses eggplant, capsicum, capers, raisins and tomatoes. I don't include raisins and capers in my caponata but, then again, every town in Sicily has their own take on this traditional dish. This is mine ...

INGREDIENTS

- 2 tablespoons **extra-virgin olive oil**
- 1 small **onion**, roughly chopped
- 2 **garlic cloves**, finely chopped
- ½ long **red chilli**, finely chopped
- 4 very **ripe tomatoes**, roughly chopped
- 1 small **eggplant (aubergine)**, roughly chopped
- 1 **red capsicum (bell pepper)**, roughly chopped
- 20 **kalamata olives**, pitted and roughly chopped
- 1 large handful **basil**, roughly chopped
- 1 teaspoon **dried oregano**
- 1 teaspoon **sugar**
- **sea salt flakes**

METHOD

Heat the olive oil in a saucepan over a medium heat. Add the onion, garlic and chilli and cook until translucent, about 3 minutes.

Add the tomatoes, eggplant and capsicum and continue to cook, stirring occasionally, until softened, about another 10 minutes.

Add the olives, basil, oregano and sugar, and cook over a low heat until it is all combined and cooked through, about another 5 minutes. Season with sea salt and freshly ground black pepper.

Marinated artichokes

{ MAKES 80 ARTICHOKE QUARTERS }

Artichokes are my favourite vegetable, so when they aren't in season, I love knowing that I have jars of them marinating in the pantry. Preserving is fabulous, as you can enjoy out-of-season produce whenever you want. These artichokes are ideal when you want to whip up a quick pasta, or use them as a pizza topping, or even a little snack on an antipasto board.

INGREDIENTS

- 20 **globe artichokes**
- juice of 1 **lemon**
- 750 ml (25½ fl oz/3 cups) **white vinegar**
- 125 ml (4 fl oz/½ cup) **white wine**
- 2–3 **bay leaves**
- 2 tablespoons **salt**
- **garlic cloves**, smashed, for storing in jars
- **chillies** for storing in jars
- **oregano** for storing in jars
- **olive oil** for storing in jars

METHOD

Peel and clean the artichokes, leaving only the hearts intact, then cut them into quarters, discarding the choke.

Cover the artichoke quarters with some water and the lemon juice in a bowl to prevent oxidisation.

Mix the vinegar, wine, bay leaves, salt and 500 ml (17 fl oz/2 cups) of water in a medium saucepan, and bring the mixture to the boil.

Put about 20 quarters of artichokes at a time in the saucepan. Cover and return to the boil, cooking for 3–4 minutes. Remove the artichokes, place them face down on clean tea towels (dish towels) and cover. Leave them overnight to dry well. Repeat with the remaining artichoke quarters.

The next day, place the artichokes in sterilised jars with garlic, chilli and oregano – use as much as takes your fancy (or suits your palate). Then cover them with olive oil and ensure there are no air bubbles. Seal tightly and store in a dry, cool place. Once sealed, these will last for months. Use as required, but refrigerate once opened. These should last a few weeks in the fridge but are best eaten fresh.

Roasted balsamic red capsicums

Roasting capsicums is one of the simplest things to do, yet such a beautiful way to add depth of flavour to a basic ingredient. I love how sweet they become, the soft texture and then the acidic hit you get from the balsamic. They're very versatile and you can use them for all sorts of things – on pizzas, in salads, with a bit of crusty bread as an antipasto, or even in pasta. Such a gorgeous recipe!

INGREDIENTS

- 4 **red capsicums (bell peppers)**
- 2 tablespoons **extra-virgin olive oil**
- 2 tablespoons **balsamic vinegar**
- **sea salt flakes**
- 50 g (1¾ oz/½ bunch) **basil**, leaves picked

METHOD

Turn the grill (broiler) on to medium heat in the oven.

Cut the capsicums in half, removing the stalk and seeds. Wash and dry well.

Place the halves on a foil-lined baking tray, skin side up and place under the grill for about 10–15 minutes. Don't be alarmed when the capsicum skins start to burn – you want them to burn so they become easy to peel away.

Remove the capsicum pieces from the tray once the skin is black and bubbled. Place in a bowl and cover with plastic wrap (so the capsicums sweat and peel easily).

Once cooled, peel the skins off the capsicums and thinly slice the flesh. Toss in a bowl with the olive oil and balsamic vinegar, season with sea salt and toss through the basil leaves.

Store in a jar or airtight container in the fridge. They will last for about 1–2 weeks.

Anchovies in oil

Anchovies are so small and delicate, yet they're packed with flavour. White anchovies are just to die for. I usually eat half the jar before I start cooking with them. When melted into a sauce, the flavour they release is just magnificent.

INGREDIENTS

- 300 g (10½ oz) **salted anchovy fillets**

- 250 ml (8½ fl oz/1 cup) **red-wine vinegar**

- 75 g (2¾ oz/½ bunch) **flat-leaf (Italian) parsley**, finely chopped

- 2 **garlic cloves**, finely chopped

- 1 **long red chilli**, finely chopped

- **extra-virgin olive oil** for storing

METHOD

Taking one anchovy at a time, use a paring knife to carefully scrape off the salt and the top layer of skin on each side.

Carefully open the fish up. Remove the fish bone and scrape out the insides, so that you are left with two clean fillets. Place them in a clean bowl. Continue to clean each anchovy, and once you have prepared them all, cover them with red-wine vinegar, then gently squeeze the excess vinegar out of the anchovies using your hands. Place on a clean plate.

Combine the parsley, garlic and chilli.

Layer the anchovies in a hard plastic container, sprinkling the parsley mixture over each layer before adding the next layer. Cover with olive oil, seal with a lid and refrigerate, using as required. These should last for several weeks.

Olives, brined and marinated

{ MAKES ABOUT 5 KG (11 LB) }

Every year we go out and pick the black kalamata olives to brine and marinate, so we have a supply for the whole year round. The process is a long one, but there is something very special and rewarding about preserving and marinating your own olives. When it's time to create your marinade, use as little or as much chilli, thyme or other fresh herbs as suits your palate.

INGREDIENTS

- 5 kg (11 lb) **black kalamata olives**

BRINE

- 1 kg (2 lb 3 oz) **salt**
- **red-wine vinegar**

METHOD

Wash the olives thoroughly and soak overnight in clean water.

Bring 10 litres (340 fl oz) of water to the boil in a large stockpot and add the salt. Boil for 5 minutes. Allow to cool completely.

Put the olives in a large container or bucket and cover them with the cooled brine. Put a heavy plate or a weight over the olives so they stay submerged in the brine, and seal with a lid.

A natural fermentation will occur, so the top of the container will need to be loosened occasionally to allow carbon dioxide to escape. During this process, you will begin to see some mould on the top of the bucket. This is normal. The brine can be changed during this time, using a fresh batch of the brine. Scrape the mould off and change the brine every 2–3 weeks if possible. The process should take about 3–4 months if the olives are kept whole. A faster way of curing olives is to slit each olive with a sharp knife first, reducing the overall process to around 6–8 weeks.

Once the olives have cured and sweetened to your liking, they are ready to be bottled. Drain and rinse well.

To store the olives, make up a fresh brine with 6% salt: boil 10 litres (340 fl oz) of water and add 600 g (1 lb 5 oz) salt.

Pack the olives into sterilised jars. Add 2 tablespoons of red wine vinegar to each jar and top with the cooled brine. (You can vary the amount of vinegar.)

Seal the jars and store in a cool, dark place until ready to use. These olives will last up to a year. Use as required, but refrigerate once opened. These should last a few weeks in the fridge but are best eaten fresh.

MARINADE

- **extra-virgin olive oil**

- **balsamic vinegar**

- **red chilli**, sliced

- **thyme sprigs** (and/or other fresh herbs)

MARINATING THE OLIVES

To marinate the olives, drain the jar and rinse the olives. In a bowl, mix the olives with some extra-virgin olive oil, a splash of balsamic vinegar, sliced chilli, thyme sprigs or any other fresh herbs you like. You can marinate them when you are ready to serve, or the marinating can be done a few days before to infuse more flavour.

MAKING FRIED OLIVES

Pour a little extra-virgin olive oil in a frying pan over a high heat, add 1 sliced garlic clove and throw in some drained olives, a few chilli slices and a splash of balsamic vinegar. Fry the olives for about 2–3 minutes – once they start to sizzle and get a little blistered, they are perfect! Serve hot.

From left to right: Napolitana, Anchovies in oil, Pesto, Olives, brined and marinated, Roasted balsamic red capsicums, Pickled mushrooms

Pickled mushrooms

{ MAKES ABOUT 550 G (1 LB 3 OZ) }

This recipe is great to have as a staple in the pantry, when mushrooms aren't in season. I love having these as an antipasto, with a bit of fresh ciabatta bread, or tossed through with some chilli and garlic as a quick pasta meal.

INGREDIENTS

- 500 g (1 lb 2 oz) **pine mushrooms** (or button mushrooms if pine mushrooms aren't available)

- 750 ml (25½ fl oz/3 cups) **white vinegar**

- 125 ml (4 fl oz/½ cup) **white wine**

- 2–3 **bay leaves**

- 1 large handful **salt**

- 1 **garlic clove**, sliced

- whole **thyme sprigs** (2–4 per jar)

- 1 large handful **flat-leaf (Italian) parsley**, chopped

- 1 **long red chilli**, finely chopped

- **extra-virgin olive oil**

METHOD

Brush and clean the mushrooms with a damp cloth. Don't cut them just yet.

In a medium saucepan, bring the vinegar, wine, bay leaves, salt and 500 ml (17 fl oz/ 2 cups) of water to the boil.

Place the mushrooms in the pickling liquid in batches. Cover and return to the boil, cooking for 3–4 minutes.

Drain the mushrooms, then slice them thinly.

When they have cooled down, divide them among 3–4 sterilised jars with some garlic, thyme, parsley and chilli. Pour over the olive oil until the mushrooms are covered.

Preserve in jars and refrigerate. These should last for a few weeks once opened, but are best eaten fresh.

Pickled green tomatoes

{ MAKES ABOUT 1 KG (2 LB 3 OZ) }

This was something I always looked forward to when Mum was able to get green tomatoes. The first time I had them I thought they'd be bitter and unpleasant, but I was blown away by how flavour-packed they were. I used to eat these pickled green tomatoes by the jar, just on crackers after school ... a rather fancy afternoon snack, I know!

INGREDIENTS

- 1 kg (2 lb 3 oz) **green tomatoes**
- **sea salt**
- **white vinegar**
- 2 **garlic cloves**, thinly sliced
- 2–3 **long red chillies**
- **extra-virgin olive oil**

METHOD

Using a mandoline, thinly slice the tomatoes. Layer them in a colander and salt every layer. Place a dinner plate on top of the tomatoes and put the colander into a large bowl. You will need to put weights on top of the dinner plate (I use a few tins).

Leave the tomatoes at room temperature for 24 hours. All the liquid will drain through the colander into the bowl.

Remove the salted tomatoes from the colander, place in a large bowl and cover with white vinegar. Leave for another 24 hours.

Remove the tomatoes from the vinegar and layer them on clean tea towels (dish towels). Roll them up and leave for 12–14 hours.

Layer the tomato slices into sterilised jars with a few slices of garlic and the chillies. Once the jars are full, cover the tomatoes with olive oil.

Seal tightly with lids and store in a dry, cool place. Once sealed, these will last for months. Use as required, but refrigerate once opened. These should last a few weeks in the fridge but are best eaten fresh.

index

a

almonds
  Amaretti biscuits 130
  Biscotti 153
  Mum's almond bread 129
  Nonna's cassatelle 126
Amaretti biscuits 130
anchovies
  Anchovies in oil 171
  Anchovy butter 74
  Beccafico 84
  Puttanesca 80
  Stuffed zucchini flowers 35
  Tomato reduction 87
aniseed
  Biscotti 153
Arancini 27
artichokes, globe
  Artichoke and pesto sauce
    50
  Chicken involtino,
    artichokes, polenta and
    caponata 107
  Beer-battered artichokes
    28
  Marinated artichokes 169
  preparing 23
  Quail with artichokes,
    mushroom panzanella
    and red wine jus 100
  Silverbeet and goat's
    cheese agnolotti with
    artichokes and pesto 50
  Stuffed artichokes (Carciofi
    ripieni) 23

b

bacon crumb 88
balsamic vinegar
  Balsamic glaze 36
  Roasted balsamic red
    capsicums 170

Basic tomato sauce
  (Napolitana) 166
basil
  Basil panna cotta 132
  Lemon and basil panna
    cotta with white
    chocolate noodles 132
  Pesto 167
  Pesto pasta with roasted
    tomato, pine nuts and
    bocconcini 54
  Tomato, buffalo curd and
    basil bruschetta 30
  Tomato, buffalo mozzarella
    and basil pizza 60
batter
  Beer-battered artichokes
    28
beans
  Cavolo nero, borlotti
    beans, polenta and
    sausages 57
Beccafico 84
beer
  Beer-battered artichokes
    28
  Chicken with beer (Pollo
    alla birra skewers) 104
biscuits
  Amaretti biscuits 130
  Biscotti 153
  Cheesecake base 145
  Mum's almond bread 129
  Savoiardi biscuits 150
blood orange
  Blood orange curd 146
  Blood orange jelly 146
  Chocolate and blood
    orange panna cotta 146
Blumenthal, Heston 83
Bowl of mussels 93
bread
  Ciabatta bread 156
  Focaccia 157

see also bruschetta
broccoli rabe
  Spaghetti with rape
    (broccoli rabe) 47
broth
  Lobster broth with
    lobster and tomato
    ravioli 79
bruschetta 156
  Mushroom and leek
    bruschetta 31
  Tomato, buffalo curd and
    basil bruschetta 30
butter 35
  Anchovy butter 74
  Herb butter 88
butter cream
  Coffee butter cream 137

c

cabbage, red
  Pickled cabbage 75
cakes
  Natalie's mocha mud
    cakes 137
Cannoli 141
capers
  Beccafico 84
  Caponata 168
  Puttanesca 80
Caponata 168
  Chicken involtino,
    artichokes, polenta
    and caponata 107
capsicum
  Caponata 168
  Roasted balsamic red
    capsicums 170
Caramelised onion 101
  Potato, caramelised
    onions and rosemary
    oil pizza 61

Rolled gnocchi with
  porcini mushrooms,
  caramelised onions
  and crispy sage 40
Carciofi ripieni (Stuffed
  artichokes) 23
Carluccio, Antonio 57
carrots
  Heirloom carrots with fennel
    and orange dressing 58
Cavolo nero, borlotti beans,
  polenta and sausages 57
cheese
  Arancini 27
  Gorgonzola, prosciutto,
    rocket and pesto pizza
    65
  Pesto pasta with roasted
    tomato, pine nuts and
    bocconcini 54
  Quail, peach, witlof,
    prosciutto and buffalo
    mozzarella salad with
    balsamic glaze 36
  Silverbeet and goat's
    cheese agnolotti with
    artichokes and pesto 50
  Stuffed zucchini flowers 35
  Tomato, buffalo mozzarella
    and basil pizza 60
  Zia Dora's famous tiramisu
    121
  see also curd; ricotta
cheesecake
  Tangy citrus cheesecakes
    145
chestnuts
  chestnut flour 19, 123
  Chestnut forest (Modern
    tiramisu) 122
  chestnut purée 123
  Quail, pine mushrooms,
    chestnuts and polenta
    108

acknowledgements

I owe this book to a million and one people, past, present and from up above.

First, to the team at Hardie Grant Publishing: I can't thank you enough for the hours you have all put in to make my dream cookbook the most perfect cookbook I have ever laid eyes on. You made this whole process one of the most enjoyable experiences, and I can't wait for round 2! A massive thank you to Paul McNally, for falling in love with my concept and making a childhood dream of mine come true. You put together the best team to work on my book and listened to every little detail I wanted. It's everything and more I ever expected this book to be. To my editor Susie Ashworth, I promised you'd have the biggest thank you of all time, so here goes ... Thank you from the absolute bottom of my heart for those extremely late nights and early morning corrections, for the most prompt responses and for putting up with my delayed ones, for every little detail and innovative idea, and for being the best editor I could have asked for. Oh, and how could I forget your patience! No joke, I would take a day to correct one recipe ... you'd do a whole chapter in half a day! You will probably need a six-month holiday away after this book – you deserve it! You're truly amazing at what you do. I can't wait to work with you in the future. So much love! My food editor, Katrina Cleary, I don't know how you put up with my guesstimates in each recipe: 'are you sure a handful of basil isn't clear enough?', 'surely everyone has the same sized hand?' You helped me perfect every recipe, to the finest detail, even cooking each recipe. Oh, and for putting up with my extremely delayed responses at times. You are a machine of a woman!

To the best crew behind the beautiful pictures, styling and design of the book: Mark Campbell, thank you for making sure the shoot week was one of the best weeks of my life. As exhausting and painful as I can be, you let me sing and dance all day long in the kitchen, which is a lot to handle! Your eye for detail is just incredible – you have made me one happy girl! I am so glad to have had you working on my book. Vicki Valsamis, aka Vik-Sta! Where do I even begin with you lady? If you can make a plate of plain tomato sauce pasta look like the Mona Lisa, then you're pretty special. I have never met someone who has such a detailed eye for perfection; each plate, piece of cutlery, tea towel, board and apron used in each shot. Oh my lord, you absolutely nailed it sister. I have no words for you ... well, maybe one. Perfection. To my photographer, Chris Middleton, you are an absolute genius at what you do. I've never seen such beautiful work before. Thank you for making each shot look a million dollars – even my horrific photobombs looked bloody decent. If you ever need a photographer, there is no one else I would recommend more highly. Natalie Homan, where should I start? You are such a talented chef, a beautiful lady and such a hard worker. Cooking all day on set, then going home and preparing food in your own time for the next day. Talk about commitment. Thank you from the bottom of my heart for helping me cook every dish, for teaching me new techniques, for the laughs, for putting up with my kitchen madness and for perfecting each recipe.

To my publicist Caitlin Neville and marketing director Roxy Ryan, thank you for your hours of hard work, for making sure this book reaches its potential (both in Australia and overseas) and for going above and beyond for me. Thank you so much to Murray Batten for creating the beautiful design in *My Italian Kitchen* – it's everything I wanted and so much more. You created a masterpiece and I am so thankful and grateful you designed my cookbook.

You've done absolute wonders. Last but not least, to the beautiful lady Hannah Koelmeyer. You have been my go-to woman for everything about this book. You've solved every little bump in the road and answered every question, from hairstyling to recipe dramas. You have honestly been the best project manager. Thank you times a million – I couldn't have done it without you!

I hope you all enjoy the beautiful work you've created in this book.

To my gorgeous friends, in Adelaide, Melbourne, all over Australia and all around the world: thank you for being true friends. You know who you all are. From the beginning, you've all made me smile and laugh, supporting me through the toughest times and being my number 1 fans through the best. I love you all dearly. To every single person I met while on *MasterChef Australia*, thanks for putting up with me, and for helping me become who I am today. My fellow contestants: you're all incredible people. Thank you for helping me grow along the way and being a part of the best experience in my life. I am forever grateful. Margie (Margaret) Bashfield, a special thank you for helping me achieve this cookbook. I'm forever grateful. To Gary Mehigan, Matt Preston and George Calombaris: thank you for believing in me and my cooking, for seeing potential, for never giving up on me and for guiding me along the way. I am forever grateful. George, a very big thank you for your never-ending support, for writing such beautiful and inspiring words in this book and for always being a phone call away. A lot of love for you three boys. To my fans, all over the world: I couldn't have done it without your support. A lot of this is owed to you all. Thank you for choosing #teamlaura. To my San Remo Family: I am honoured to be part of such an awesome family. Thank you for the support, time and effort you have given me with this book. I am forever grateful. To two very special guys at Restaurant Orana, Jock Zonfrillo (boss man) and Shannon Fleming: thank you for taking me under your wing, for teaching me a whole new world of food, for your support, your guidance, your advice, your belief and for understanding my 'complicated' lifestyle. Lots of love, Lozza.

And, of course, to my family: you are all amazing. Your support has been just unbelievable. My cousins, my Zias and Zios, family friends, angels up above and my Nonni. Thank you for helping me become '*la regina della cucina*'. To my beautiful parents, Sandro and Anita, and the best brother and sister in the world, Aidan and Natalie: you are the driving force behind everything I've done and everything I do, the heart and brains in every project and the best people I get to come home to every day. I don't know any other family as crazy as us … yes, we fight, but we're a pretty cool bunch. You have allowed me to follow my heart and do what I love. You have supported every decision, cleaned every cut, healed every bruise and wiped away every tear. You have shaped me into the brightest version of me that I can be. You have created everything I have. Thank you. I love you all.

Please enjoy *My Italian Kitchen*.

Love always,
Laura Cassai

Published in 2015 by Hardie Grant Books

Hardie Grant Books (Australia)
Ground Floor, Building 1
658 Church Street
Richmond, Victoria 3121
www.hardiegrant.com.au

Hardie Grant Books (UK)
5th & 6th Floors
52-54 Southwark Street
London SE1 1UN
www.hardiegrant.co.uk

A Cataloguing-in-Publication entry is available from
the catalogue of the National Library of Australia
at www.nla.gov.au

My Italian Kitchen
ISBN 9781743790021

Publishing Director: Paul McNally
Project Editor: Hannah Koelmeyer
Editor: Susie Ashworth
Food Editor: Katrina Cleary
Design Manager: Mark Campbell
Designer: Murray Batten
Photographer: Chris Middleton
Stylist: Vicki Valsamis
Home Economist: Natalie Homan
Production Manager: Todd Rechner

Colour reproduction by
Splitting Image Colour Studio
Printed and bound in China by
1010 Printing International Limited

Find this book on **Cooked.**
cooked.com.au | cooked.co.uk